The Man from Brazil

Volume 1

Dorothy Griffin's Diary

(1942-43)

Virginia Dickinson (Editor)

ARC Publishing

ISBN 978-0-9935613-2-0 (Paperback)

Published by ARC Publishing (Karen Slee)

Old Tavern House,
Riding Mill,
Northumberland,
England
NE44 6DX

DEDICATION

This book is dedicated to Mother and Father; the loving couple portrayed in these pages as two twenty something year olds, travelling an incredible journey in life together, never holding back their offspring. Thank you for your support.

ACKNOWLEDGEMENTS

No man is an island, we achieve little without encouragement, and we surely need plenty when embarking on such an idea.

My grateful thanks to Raymond Slee for his interest and enthusiasm in this without his help I would have floundered.

Thank you also to my daughter Patricia and family for listening, reading, and not discouraging this vanity project.

Many thanks to ARC Publishing, David and Karen Slee who have made the transition from typed pages into printed pages.

The diary, letters and photos are the purpose of this book, and a "Muito Obrigada, mano gemeo" goes to my twin brother, Christopher, for saving them and showing them to me back in 2004, when we celebrated our 60th birthday.

PREFACE

This Diary was written in 1942-43 by Dorothy Griffin. The entries have a resemblance to today's tweets: short, to the point, and sometimes enigmatic. I learned much from typing it, not just the intimate thoughts of a 21-year-old, hot blooded English woman during WWII, but also many of the expressions of the time all but now redundant. Several had me puzzled for weeks, and I owe a very big thank you to the contributors of Rootschat.com for their excellent help.

Virginia Dickinson
November 2016

1942			JANUARY			1942
M	T	W	T	F	S	S
..	..	..	1	2	3	4
5	6	7	8	9	10	11
12	13	14	15	16	17	18
19	20	21	22	23	24	25
26	27	28	29	30	31	..

January 1st

Omitted (must've been very virtuous!)

January 13th

Rah! Rah! RAH! RAH! RAH! Grand news – passed the selection board (Yorkshire – November) leaving Bridgnorth[1] shortly – "at an early date" for a bomber station – "hush-hush" job. Must tell everyone!

---

[1] RAF Bridgnorth: From August 1941 to September 1942 known as "No. 1 Women's Auxiliary Air Force Depot" where WAAF recruits were trained.

January 17th

Last minute decision – hitched to Oxford to Peggy and the new sergeant. Horrified to hear that her name is – "Effie". 'Strewth! Good going until we found an interesting looking pub 10 miles from Oxford. After 5 sherries and a beer gaily sailed along the road: arrived there five hours late.

January 18th

After a restless night with that hefty wench, Peggy, awoke to find Oxford more beautiful than ever – snow everywhere. Afternoon in Tony's rooms – drinking beer: and sipping brandy: guzzling tea: walked around Addison's Walk[1].

January 30th

Wonderful day of anticipation and realisation! Bath, lunch and then to Wolverhampton for the 1435 to London – and Michael. Actually arrived two hours early! Whiled away the time talking to the lavatory attendant at Waterloo. And then Michael – dear, dear Michael. Rooms in a discreet little hotel: drinks in the Strand "Temple Bar": sausage and mash at 1.30 in the morning: chasing around Nelson's column hunting for a taxi. . . and then humming the tune of the moment – I haven't said thanks for the lovely weekend.

---

[1] A picturesque footpath around an island in the River Cherwell in the grounds of Magdalen College, Oxford.

January 31st

What a night! I spent the morning furtively peering in mirrors to see if there was any visible alterations . . . I have still not been seduced, damn it! But there's time –nights and nights of wonder and discovery - and loving.... Down to Hampshire at lunchtime. Duly admired the recently acquired red M.G. (the "Beetle") whizzed down to Petersfield[1] in it and when we halted, were immediately surrounded by hoards of admiring small boys.

[1] Petersfield: a market town in East Hampshire

1942 FEBRUARY 1942

M	T	W	T	F	S	S
..	..	..	..	..	..	1
2	3	4	5	6	7	8
9	10	11	12	13	14	15
16	17	18	19	20	21	22
23	24	25	26	27	28	..

February 1st

Peaceful night – no fault of Michael's he behaves rather well under his stepmother's vigilant eye. Had hoped to return to town in the Beetle but after frantically sweeping the snow away from the drive the damn machine refused even to cough or splutter. . .

February 2nd

Survived the Guard's eagle eyed scrutiny of my pass: eight hours overdue. Feel tired but so happy. Michael – my second, my last and my dearest love... ever always and eternally.

February 6th

Immensely cheered by a letter from Michael. The poor dear was in a mixed frame of mind. Desperately in love (he says so!) and simply livid because he's had to do some snow shovelling – coal-heaver – snow shoveller: any old thing – he's still Michael – the same Michael – my beloved Michael.

February 8th

Another wonderful letter. Michael is waking up. He's feeling so sorry for himself as he has a cold. He will probably survive. Still love him – always shall, with or without a cold!

February 17th

Heigh, ho! What a night. First Oxford where I drank brandy & beer & coffee in Tony's rooms. Stayed so late that we had to climb out of Magdalen. Were spotted by RAF S.P.'s who flashed the lights at us and it was all very thrilling.

February 18th

Home after a night in the train. Ended up at the wrong railway station in Southampton: spent an hour careering around bleary eyed & haggard in a rattling old train.

February 20th

Merchant Navy brother's ship in port: done his damndest to persuade me to stay at home tomorrow as Geoff is home but – the call of Michael is stronger, so – heigh-ho for Liss[1] tomorrow.

February 21st

'Gram[2] from Michael: can't arrange weekend. Let off steam by drinking limited quantities of alcohol, aided and abetted by George, Geoff & Johnnie. High spot – George & I started a fight with some soldiers, but Geoff dragged George away, and Johnnie led me away. Oh! The frustration of it! Johnnie was amorous.

---

[1] Liss, a small village in Hampshire, in the South Downs.

[2] 'Gram, short for telegram.

February 22nd

Hours speeding by – almost time for the dreary walk to the station and then – 12 hours in the train, and the hateful Midlands once again.

February 23rd

Usual rude letter from Aubrey (of Malta).

1942			MARCH			1942
M	T	W	T	F	S	S
..	..	..	..	..	..	1
2	3	4	5	6	7	8
9	10	11	12	13	14	15
16	17	18	19	20	21	22
23/30	24/31	25	26	27	28	29

March 9th

Dear Scranny has popped up again! He's depressed and hates South Africa – but he's found some consolation: the fact that her mother is a Scotswoman and a Presbyterian seems to be the main drawback!

March 13th

Ha! Aubrey again – this time addressing me as "fair lady of many stripes". Just wait until I grab a pen and a few score sheets of airmail paper.

March 19th

Wonderfully long 'gram from Michael, practically ordering me to go to Liss as he's on special leave. Ha! How dare he!! I resent his arrogance and his demanding ways. . .

March 24th

Heigh-ho for Hampshire and Michael. Frightfully confused about trains at Birmingham so – I didn't arrive in town until too late. Phoned Mrs. M.B. who wasn't at all surprised.

March 25th

Spent a gloomy (but virtuous) night in a Salvation Army hostel. Succumbed to irresistible desire to "hitch": consequently did not arrive at Liss until lunch time. Met by a very tired – but oh so attractive looking Michael.

Changed into slacks, etc at the earliest opportunity and spent the afternoon in the sunshine. And the night? – spent in the happiest way I know – in Michael's arms – at least until 4 a.m. when he returned to his own bedroom, discretion being the better part of something or other. We behaved awfully well, though, and the Imp. Virg. is still a virgin – but becoming more and more excited every night.

March 26th

After very blasé farewell – horribly frigid – Michael hopped onto the train (which went so quickly that there just wasn't time to wave) and I staggered across to the waiting room to indulge in a spot of furious weeping. I hitched to Dorset later.

March 27th

Peaceful night in my own virginal bed. Refused to accept the cold fact that Michael is going overseas. Went to a funny film which made me feel happier – though not much. Brother – merchant navy – left Dorset 2 days ago for America.

March 28th

After a night's travelling, spent a nightmarish day looking haggard and feeling hellish. Bloody life!

1942			APRIL			1942
M	T	W	T	F	S	S
..	..	1	2	3	4	5
6	7	8	9	10	11	12
13	14	15	16	17	18	19
20	21	22	23	24	25	26
27	28	29	30	..	..	..

April 3rd

Such a letter from Michael – so sweet, so touching. Well, he's kept me waiting so long for some of his beastly little letters that I think it's time I adopted his technique. I will reserve a rear corner – a very rear corner of my mind for him.

April 4th

Sunshine outside – but tears inside. I felt depressed – behaved shockingly. Wept all over the place. "Effie" has promised to take action about my posting. Heigh ho!!!!!

April 5th

Interesting – very interesting... Whilst quaffing beer at the "Crown" met someone called Richard: very nice. Brown eyes, nice chin – yes! Definitely worth knowing.

April 9th

Ha! Michael is waking up. Another letter – this time he pours out his heart in the dramatic way he does most things, and then ends up by making the sinister suggestion that I am still in love with South American Joe and has the damned cheek to wish us both the best of luck – blasted effrontery.

April 10th

Today, I sent my reply to Michael. I do hope that he's waiting for it – and that it hurts him – conceited, arrogant, pig-headed young fool. I've confided in him – yes, the awful truth – that I despise him and the snobbish superficial social-climbing atmosphere in which he's been brought up. I hate myself, too.

April 24th

Heavenly reams – long letter from Scranny. Tenderly enquires about the legs – which, say he, are two of the 101 things a young man should see! I wonder, who owns the other fifty legs, and – who has the odd one?

April 25th

Wonderful day! Accompanied by Madge and Peggy, left camp this afternoon – they for London, I for Dorset. Rode on the back of a rattling old lorry: stopped at an inn in Zummerset and dropped P. & M. at Marlborough, Wilts. I arrived home at 1.0 am, after having covered the last two miles on the carrier of a pickled soldier's bike and then on an air raid warden's mo' bike.

April 26th

The inevitable film with the inevitable companions – my mother, Peggy (bro's girl-friend) and the Pest in Long Pants. Very dull – but a change.

April 27th

Walked to the beach: met various people: glorious sunshine – bloody war – hateful 1942!

1942			MAY			1942
M	T	W	T	F	S	S
..	..	..	..	1	2	3
4	5	6	7	8	9	10
11	12	13	14	15	16	17
18	19	20	21	22	23	24
25	26	27	28	29	30	31

May 3rd

Lovely day of freedom! Sailed out of camp with mufti in small case: changed into slacks and sweater at Quatford Castle[1]: lounged in the fields with the ever faithful Richard.

May 7th

Gram from Johnnie – embark. leave. I no can do until next Tuesday. Hope he's still in Dorset then.

May 11th

Correct 'gram arrived from Johnnie. His leave ends today. Hell! But I'll go home tomorrow just the same – I'm in urgent need of it. Saw Richard, who, if what he says is true, will be a pining skeleton when I return.

---

[1] Quatford Castle – A mock castle built c1830 adjacent to the River Severn about 2 miles from Bridgnorth.

May 12th

Found last month's copy of "Men Only"[1]. First thing I read was "Hitch-Hiking Around Europe" by a bloke called Leishman. Decided to write to him, to get a spot of gen on the matter.

May 13th

Travelled all night: arrived at lunch-time. Slept this afternoon – fearfully tired: terribly hard-up. Amusing 'gram from dear old Aubrey in Malta – old devil.

May 14th

Great excitement – M.N. bro' home from America, with all sorts of souvenirs and good things to eat: outrageous American sweaters and such an American accent. Whole house in an uproar.

May 15th

Wired Bridgnorth for an extension: spent the evening at the local cinema (hah!) with the mater and George's girl friend.

May 16th

Filthy day! Beastly letter from Johnnie (now in Cheshire): 'gram from B... who want to know the whys and wherefores of everything. Hell. I'm on the verge of rebellion. Sent express letter to J. and restrained 'gram to B. Bought a rather wiz edition of "Omar Khayyam."

---

[1] A pocket men's magazine with a stated editorial policy: 'We don't want women readers. We won't have women readers...' It sought 'bright articles on current male topics'. The magazine carried colour paintings of 'art' nudes.

May 17th

My 21st! Feel rather peeved about spending it so tamely. Everyone's in a filthy mood – bickering, squabbling and throwing things. One greetings' gram and also favourable reply from Bridgnorth – the blighters.

May 18th

Enjoyed myself – change! Spent afternoon at symphony concert and later bought Peter Fleming's "Brazilian Adventure." Met the mater[1] and saw Carmen Miranda's latest film; came out feeling drunk with colour & music. More greetings 'grams.

May 19th

Accompanied by the fam.[2], went to the flicks. There was something in the film about horses being killed to manufacture glue – couldn't resist stuffing Pest Minor that they do the same with small boys (America - of course!). He's absolutely disgusted.

May 20th

Terrific shopping orgy. Bought some wizard notepaper initialled 'D' and also a copy of the long-coveted "Poems from the Forces." Express letter from Johnnie – very penitent: and a cake from the aunts in Bristol.

---

[1] Public school slang for mother.

[2] Short for "family"

May 21st

Farewell to the Merchant Navy! Bro' left for Glasgow at lunchtime. We were all cheerfully rude and solemnly saluted each other in the approved thumb-to-nose fashion.

May 22nd

Camp at 8.0 am., after thirteen dreary hours in stuffy trains and depressing waiting-rooms. Brightened up considerably when I found several intriguing-looking envelopes, a 'gram and a parcel. There were two books from the two mad men of Magdalen (who, I thought had passed out of my life forever) – Tony and Donald, and book tokens value a guinea from my beloved Hags. Three letters in this morning's mail – one from that interesting person Vince, who's about to become a sub. Lieut.

May 23rd

Phoned my dear Kathleen, who has asked me to spend a weekend in Penarth[1]. Think I will – she seems very sad – badly in need of a pep-talk. Johnnie rang up and we've made some fairly satisfactory arrangements. I'm to meet him in Cheshire on Monday.

May 24th

Slaving away all day. Passed several more enchanting hours engrossed in "Brazilian Adventure." Another phone call from Cheshire – he's sailing today. I'm rather sorry...

---

[1] A town in the Vale of Glamorgan, Wales, at the southern end of Cardiff Bay.

May 25th

Peculiar day – stayed in bed: missed meals: occasionally hopped out, to make tea and spend pennies. Horribly restful.

May 26th

Frightfully dramatic letter from Johnnie – all about dense jungles and burning deserts. How funny if he ends up in some civilized hole – he will be disappointed!

May 28th

Letter and a half-a-crown from the mater. Bloody Jerries have been busy over Dorset again. Damn them!! Also the book – "Poems from the Forces" from the peculiar Spanish-countess woman with blonde hair and green eyelids.

May 29th

Saw the most wonderful film – 'planes and Chopin's Military Polonaise and the "Warsaw Concerto." Came out of the dreary camp cinema walking on air, living in a world of music. Visited the "Crown" and drank beer (bought by a very jolly captain – Army) who was either frightfully Etonian (or terribly pickled) and still in a dream, met Richard (my local love) again.

May 30th

Further intriguing letter from Vince. I think – I hope – I shall be meeting him soon. Poor Kathleen has sent me a letter from the Red Cross – there's very slight hope that Billy will ever turn up – seven months since he was missing over Norway.

May 31st

Went all domesticated today. All part of my new resolution. Spent several hours with Rupert and Richard in the "Crown", going gay on beer, gin-and-lime and rum. Felt very merry and rather sentimental.

1942			JUNE			1942
M	T	W	T	F	S	S
1	2	3	4	5	6	7
8	9	10	11	12	13	14
15	16	17	18	19	20	21
22	23	24	25	26	27	28
29	30	..	..	..	..	..

June 3rd

Such glorious sunshine! Such wonderful sunbathing! Feel quite nauseatingly healthy.

June 4th

Birthday present from Michael – a butterfly brooch which, as far as I can gather, was flown over direct from the H.E. Met Gillian at the Station tonight. Dined at her hotel and later visited a W/O and spouse at their flat. Whiskey – but not enough of it, also, another super meal. Returned to the Derwent at midnight but G.N. squared the duty NCO. Useful woman, G.N.

June 5th

Delightful letter from Alan ("Scranny") Baker. Wants Jane, Michael and I (and of course, little "Scranny", too) to meet after the war to discuss the temptations which beset those people who sleep with attractive members of the opposite sex without seducing them – or being seduced. Late afternoon, set out on the long journey to Penarth. Foul road, no traffic, stayed in Ludlow for the night.

June 6th

Ambled through Ludlow after a good breakfast, feeling very happy. An amiable American and his mistress (charming couple) gave me a lift and stood me lunch in Newport. Found Kathleen very subdued and rather morbid. Together we saw Noel Coward's "Hayfever", and laughed a lot.

June 7th

Morning in bed: afternoon sunbathing. Decided to postpone returning to camp until tomorrow. Preparing water-tight alibi. Kathleen pathetically hauling out Billy's blazer and huge sandals, bought just before his disappearance. She seems happier.

June 8th

Hasty breakfast: rushed into Cardiff to haul K., out of her beastly little recruiting office. Hopped off the train at Hereford and leisurely "hitched" back to Bridgnorth, where I saw a funny film. One of my cronies carried my suspicious looking case, and everything was oka-da-poke.

June 9th

'Strewth! A telegram from Peter. Query – who's Peter? I think he's the one who refers to me as the "baked beans and Beethoven" girl. Apparently he 'phoned on Saturday, too, and so did Richard. Ha! Letter from Ronald (Fleet Air Arm): the beast is at Birmingham and has been for some time. "Auld acquaintance" – my aunt Fanny!

June 10th

Bunged off a rude letter to Ronald. Not sufficient energy to hike into Bridgnorth so I listened to Beethoven's 7th instead – far more satisfying way of spending an evening, methinks!

June 11th

Tonight, I listened to Schubert's 5th, and felt very mournful. No money, no Richard, no fun. The prospect of spending a weekend in camp is overwhelmingly browned-off making.

June 12th

Depressing letter from the mater. I have visions of relations' behaviour during raids – aunts fainting; cousin throwing fits: frightfully dramatic, but rather pathetic, too. Was delighted when "Nicky" invited me to drinks with her and her husband. Hugh is a darling – very quiet, tolerant and so shy.

June 13th

Felt hilarious when "Nickie" asked me to dinner at the "Crown". Hugh was just as kind and N., continually pulled his leg about his non-existent (I think!) two chins and nine stomachs. That horrible little waiter-man, Billy, was much impressed by Hugh's three rings." Ha! Damn' little provincial snob.

June 14th

'nother phone call from "Nickie" – this time – invite to lunch. I was in the bath when the call came thro', but I very quickly hopped out, climbed into clothes (and someone's borrowed collar!) and sped into Bridgnorth. After lunch, went to Wolves, to wish Hugh Godspeed. Yes! Commander Hugh Nicholson of the "Ajax" is a very nice bloke – AND HOW!!

June 15th

Gillian's (Nicky) farewell tea eggs and tomatoes – wartime treat. Cakes were stale. Later met Richard who escorted me to the flicks, and insisted on my using his handkerchief. Letter from the pompous Ronald.

June 16th

Hilarious epistle from the "Empress of the Hags." She's taken me literally and really thinks that I'd intended to book a room for us on Friday. 'Strewth! – I who had a frightfully sticky job in persuading one of the women to lend me the price of a birthday 'gram to my mother.

June 17th

Gillian N. left today. Assisted her with her unhealthy amount of luggage. I shall miss her: good influence although she unsettles me. Unsatisfactory evening – drinking with Maria Davies and some peculiar pilot she had in tow: accomplished something – told her she was a pseudo-Bohemian. Ha!

June 18th

Everyone loves me! Letter from the Mater: one from Casanova's girl-friend: another from Johnny – on the sea: and dear "Scranny".

June 19th

Evening with Richard. Both very morbid. He's passing through a difficult phase, methinks. Stayed in Peggy's bunk until midnight, working off steam. She's a very dear person.

June 20th

Heigh-ho! Off to London with a fa-la-la! Met by the "Empress" and "Scatty" at Paddington. Swept them off to Waterloo and they remembered that Kay arrived at P. Fearful scramble for a taxi: disgustingly dainty tea at some "refained"[1] joint: drinks at some other weird place: dinner somewhere else: and more drinking at the "Universal Brasserie". Scatty left at midnight. The grim woman at the King George etc., club was very disapproving: we were two hours late in.

June 21st

Grim female of last night even worse at breakfast. Have an almost overwhelming desire to bang her bottom and bawl "Bung Ho! My little lotus-blossom!" Meandered around deserted London streets and sunbathed at Kew this afternoon.

---

[1] Mocking accent: "refined"

June 22nd

Sluggish as ever – awful system: didn't leave until lunchtime. Two wrecks in uniform arrived at Griffin mansions in the evening. Hordes of obscure relations in the house: introductions all round. Before leaving town, bought four wonderful books.

June 23rd

The most perfect day – rather spoiled by a few unfortunate mishaps to K., sunbathed at Sandbanks[1]; drank iced milk; swam in the evening; really wonderful until K. dived onto the point of an anchor; not serious.

June 24th

To a film in Bournemouth; dull thing about an American suburban family. Also a grim film about the German atrocities in Russia – ghastly but necessary: the British public is still asleep – or, at least, the majority are. Found two readdressed letters from Bnorth: one from A\S\O, Gillian Nicholson. Ha!

June 25th

Window-shopping: horribly dissatisfying. Saw the wonderful "Dangerous Moonlight" film again, and someone on the stage played the Warsaw Concerto. Tonight we read poetry: I delved into my newly-acquired "Anthology of World Poetry."

---

[1] Sandy beach on a small spit of land at the mouth of Poole Harbour in Dorset.

June 26th

Numerous maddening hindrances: infuriatingly long queues; hateful holiday-makers – blast 'em! Wandered around Studland[1] and had a very unsatisfying tea. I want to bite someone!

June 27th

K. and I spend the morning buying flowers and cemetery-hunting but we couldn't find Paddy Martin's grave! But we spend a very amusing half-hour listening to a cemetery- caretaker 'phoning fellow bod–buriers enquiring if they'd buried a "party called Martin." Spent the afternoon swimming and then squelched around in the mud searching for cockles at Whitecliff[2]: found two dozens. Drinking at the "Fleets" tonight: mother rather pickled.

June 28th

Farewell to K. with her enormous amount of luggage and masses of corn-flowers presented to her by my amorous young brother. My train leaves this evening: pip-pip is escorting me to the station.

June 29th

Bloody Bridgnorth! Returned to find some crafty little sproggie in charge. Where – o where is the super Effie? – the prince of NCO's?!? Old drinking partner, A|S|O. Beryl H-B., now Asst. Adj! in my wing Hah! Fun and games! Ho! Ho!

---

[1] Village on the Isle of Purbeck in Dorset.

[2] Area of Poole, Dorset adjacent to Parkstone Bay.

June 30th

Weird letter from the morbid Eileen Williams, now at Horsham, Sussex. Odd creature!!

1942			JULY			1942
M	T	W	T	F	S	S
..	..	1	2	3	4	5
6	7	8	9	10	11	12
13	14	15	16	17	18	19
20	21	22	23	24	25	26
27	28	29	30	31	..	..

July 1st

Letters from Yvonne of the BBC., and also Aubrey Hart – only taken nine days from Malta! Beryl stood me eggs on toast at the "Cavalier" and later, we had drinks with Richard. Maddeningly peaceful evening – gathering foxgloves. I think Richard's sex-urge is practically non-existent.

July 2nd

I wonder where Michael is? Almost three months since he sailed: I ought to have heard something... anything.... Oh! Hell!

July 3rd

Discontented possessor of two measly guineas! Must get some promotion. I feel very morbid and forsaken; so dismal and forgotten. Oh! For an unexpected telegram!

July 4th

Teeming with rain: farewell to hopes of playing tennis. Saw a feeble film. Later wandered into the Salvation Army hut: saw a very aged American Army officer teaching a WAAF to play "Chatanooga Choo-Choo" on a mouth organ.

July 5th

On duty all day. Beryl continually hopping in and out. Numerous Americans in khaki meandering around. They're most disappointing – very average: not to be compared with Englishmen – or Irishmen...

July 6th

Working... working... the whole damn' time – until 22:30 hours tonight. Smoking like hell, the whole time. Must give up something: can't afford anything!!

July 7th

Say nothing! Say nothing!! An airgraph from his Lordship – Michael Moor-Bergin!!! All about himself – what he's been seeing – and the luscious fruits he's been guzzling. To tea with Beryl tonight and then – a rather good film: Mark Hambourg playing Tchaikovsky's Pianoforte Concerto.

July 8th

Such an evening! Eggs and toast at the "Cavalier" with Peggy and Madge, and then – a terrific drinking session with Richard and co., Jim and Jessie wandered into the woods and R., and I indulged in a spot of pash[1]., in the back of the car.

July 9th

Duty all day – and all night. Hastily scrawled a letter to the ever-tolerant Kathleen: worked frightfully hard. Sent a 'gram to Peggie F., whose birthday was yesterday, methinks!

July 10th

Tonight was wonderful – the London Symphony playing the "Leonora" overture, and – the "Pastoral". K. 'phoned from Wales: hope to meet in Shrewsbury on Sunday.

July 11th

The faithful and oh so patient! Richard spent this afternoon teaching me how to wham tennis balls into the kitchen garden of Quatford Castle. With this dashing about and a Herculean struggle with the zips on my shorts, I feel an utter wreck (1st class!)

July 12th

'nother terrific feat – cycled to Shrewsbury. K. and I met some Americans – and how! The one I like is an absolute darling – loves Beethoven and cynical poetry. Drank beer, see-sawed in a children's playground: decided to postpone my return to camp.

---

1 Passion.

July 13th

If I were more youthful – or less experienced? – I should blush with shame. Spent the night on the river – in a borrowed punt – whose? – then – drinking tea on the station: making love in an empty train: more tea : washing dishes in a canteen. The boys deserted us at 0600 hours – with many promises. Crawled back to camp on the old bike: had coffee in the "Cav"; Ghastly news! The adjutant absolutely frantic – thought I'd been assaulted (what a hope!): had 'phoned Shrewsbury Police – oh Lord!! Says she could weep with relief at the sight of me.

July 14th

On charge today! Reeled off my alibi like a well-trained parrot. C.O., very lenient – admonished me: didn't even tear off a strip! I'll take a very dim view of the Shrewsbury Police if they send in a report about me. Strewth.

July 15th

A belated reply to a January letter arrived from Yvonne Osborne – ex-B.B.C. now training as a nurse – present duties, taking care of crotchety old women and squawking brats.

July 16th

Simply livid! Hared off to Wolves[1] – loathsome dump. No Buddy! Shook me badly. Picked up (ha!) by a revolting little airman who bought me some beer. Feel fed to the teeth.

[1] Wolverhampton.

July 17th

Cheerfully assured everyone that I had the most wonderful time last night. Grhh! I'll sock the first American I meet!

July 18th

Very dejectedly climbed into one of the trucks and went to dance at the American camp. Only bright spot was the hillbilly music, until - at 10:30 I found Buddy. A Scotsman - doctor, I believe - gave us a lift into the enchanted town of Shrewsbury. Found Kathleen and stayed at a hateful hostel with her.

July 19th

Left the ghastly hotel at the earliest possible moment. Met my love at lunchtime: he'd dug up a most peculiar Yank protruding teeth and pimps - for K., she was livid. Most depressing evening in Wolves but - whew! What a night - on the station. A snack bar stung us most shockingly for a measly meal so we removed the notices from the windows.

July 20th

Feeling ill thru lack of sleep. Bed at 18:00 hours.

July 21st

Fourteen hours sleep! Shades of my distant youth! 'Phone calls from both Buddy and Richard. Letter from the Mater with airgraph from George - who's bored stiff with life - or lack of it - on the "Aquitania"[1].

---

[1] A Cunard liner converted to a troop carrier during WWII; during this period employed in transporting American troops to England in convoy.

July 22nd

Frantically pedalled over the hills in Wellington to meet Buddy. He's rather keen on that delicate conversation – topic – holy matrimony.

July 23rd

Feeling thoroughly dejected: went out for a meal with May and Marion. Afterwards, saw a second-rate film that I'd been bored with before. Heard Vince's sister is on the camp. Curious to see her. Vince is a pig.

July 24th

Accidentally met Richard tonight. Frightfully morbid. Everyone is so difficult, and life is horribly complicated. Oh me!

July 25th

On duty at the Guard Rm., - loathsome job. After a few gentle hints, the S.P's. offered me some salmon and a mug of tea.

July 26th

Such a depressing day! It rained and there was nowhere to eat. How I hate Wolverhampton – and like Buddy even more....

July 27th

It's raining: it's cold; I feel ill: everyone is bad-tempered. Letters from K., - and the temperamental Richard. 'Phone call from Richard. Feel a trifle knock - kneed about the exam, tomorrow.

July 28th

Fun and games at the exam thing. Gave the most ridiculous answers. Don't give a damn! Try again in November!! Parcel from the Mater – tomatoes and fudge; cable from Johnnie. Letter from scatty Beryl.

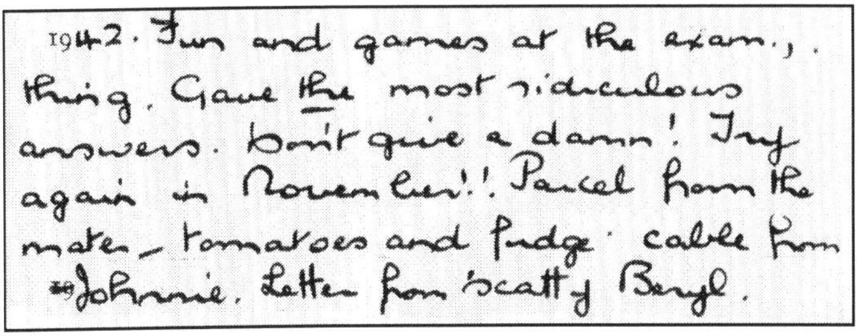
1942. Fun and games at the exam., .
thing. Gave the most ridiculous
answers. Don't give a damn! Try
again in November!. Parcel from the
mater – tomatoes and fudge · cable from
Johnnie. Letter from scatty Beryl.

July 29th

Typing test – the most hopeless mess. Eager to see Richard so didn't worry. R. quite bowled over by the sight of his little mare leaping around in the briefest of sun-suits.

July 30th

Too exhausting! More leaping around on the Quatford tennis-court. Last night, according to R., I was "putrid", tonight, I am "improving". He says that I'd make an ideal wife. Quite quite irrelevant....

July 31st

Heavenly sunshine. Relaxed in sun-suit outside the hut, trying to concentrate on darning – how I hate it!!

1942			AUGUST			1942
M	T	W	T	F	S	S
..	..	..	..	..	1	2
3	4	5	6	7	8	9
10	11	12	13	14	15	16
17	18	19	20	21	22	23
24/31	25	26	27	28	29	30

August 1st

Card from Buddy – very formal "greetings from the Isle of Man." Gillian N. has sent me such a cute swimsuit. One sunny afternoon, I'll dash down to the swimming pool in it – and risk the consequences! Richard and Rupert escorted me to the one and only cinema tonight. I wish Buddy would write – a long and intriguing letter....

August 2nd

Call from Richard. Too dull to swim. Collected a very miserable Peggy and took her out to tea and then to a film. Met Richard and Rupert: Peggy and I tight. Peggy involved with an American who, say she, has such a personality that she'd cheerfully surrender to him!!

August 3rd

Foul day – absolutely foul. I'm working: it's raining and I'm cold. Also, no-one's written to me. Dashed off a few letters to people.

August 4th

Hah! Letter from Buddy – written on stationery with the inspiring crest – "Return with Honour"... Thinking of me – quite a bit (or so he says!) Hastily scribbled a rather nasty reply. I am an unpleasant little beast.

August 5th

Richard took me to a film: beautiful colours but very childish. Found Peggy in the "Crown" – half-seas over. Rescued her from the clutches of a New Zealander and escorted her back to camp.

August 6th

Guard Room duty – again. Snaffled numerous sandwiches when the SP's were looking the other way....

August 7th

Such a sweet letter from the foolish Richard. Some SP's bought beer for Peggy and I tonight. Spent our remaining money on chips: swindled the man out of 7d. No sign of Richard. Feel in urgent need of him.

August 8th

God! But how fed up I am! Weird, incoherent letter from the Mater. Dopey cousin Doris has a baby – poor little brat!

August 9th

Richard involved with relations: I went to the camp flicks with a gang of women. Film old – very, very old...

August 10th

Tomatoes and apples, cigarettes and half-a-crown from the mater. AND two long letters from Michael M-B. His sense of humour is improving but I don't think I love him. Dear, foolish Michael.

August 11th

Frantically sewing the "old goonie" (Scots for nightie!) God knows what it'll look like when it's finished. All the women are giving me advice and eyeing it critically.

August 12th

Drill – or dentist? Decided on the lesser of the two evils: nothing happened, made an appointment for next week.

August 13th

Buddy phoned – very breathless –dashing off to London. Ha!

August 14th

Met Richard. Read Housman's "Shropshire Lad" in the "Crown". I don't think I like it particularly. Looking at Richard – the straight nose, the perfect chin, the gay, kind brown eyes, I feel a vague unpleasant sense of guilt.

August 15th

Heigh-ho for London – and Buddy... Two hours late. He's moved to Kent: had to crawl thro' barbed wire to get out. Ate, drank at the Universalle Brasserie. Wandered around the wet, crowded streets and – eventually – reached Victoria.

August 16th

Spent the night sitting outside Victoria like two old flower-sellers.

 - like this. It wasn't a real seat.

Buddy excited me - but nothing worth-while mentioning happened - how could it? - outside Victoria??... in the rain?? A policeman was suspicious. Went to Dorset at lunch-time; rowed with my father who described Americans as "b-y Yanks." Thundering, prejudiced cheek! Mother as sweet as ever. Sunshine - glorious after dismal London.

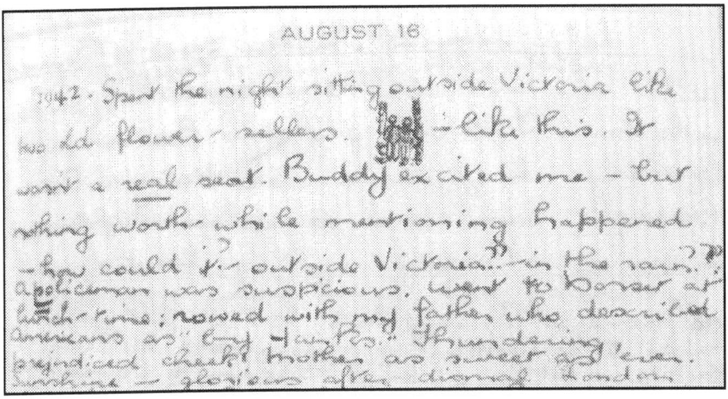

AUGUST 16

1942. Spent the night sitting outside Victoria like
wo old flower-sellers. - like this. It
wasn't a real seat. Buddy excited me - but
nothing worth-while mentioning happened
- how could it? - outside Victoria?? in the rain??
A policeman was suspicious. Went to Dorset at
lunch-time; rowed with my father who described
Americans as "b-y Yanks." Thundering,
prejudiced cheek! Mother as sweet as ever.
Sunshine - glorious after dismal London

August 17th

Lazy morning. Mother came to Bournemouth with me and I bought "This Above All" and read 200 – something pages in the train. Felt very gay and free in mufti[1]. Blithely whizzed across to Victoria. No Buddy!! – Sam came to explain. Fighters on ops, so – Buddy working. Went down to Bromley and drank beer – very slowly – no money. B., very late, but I felt quite happy. He's written some words to his music – title: "My Wonderful Dream's Come True". Sam thinks it's extremely good – but he's prejudiced - great admirer of Buddy's. Buddy came to town with me, and I loaned him half-a-crown to stay at the "Washington". Is this known as "versa vice"?

August 18th

Camp at 8.0 a.m. Everybody making discreet enquiries about seduction. Too lazy to draw upon my imagination. They've all won their bets – that means that I have to stand Beryl eggs-on-toast : Marion, half-a-beer. Letters from Johnnie, Scatty – and darling Scranny with a very happy photo.

August 19th

Odd sort of letter from my "very amorous Richard" (his own words). He feels that something is coming between us. I wonder - has he a premonition or is he merely being funny?

---

[1] Plain clothes worn by a person who wears a uniform for their job.

August 20th

Stupid lecture from "Stoogie" Sprules: she picturesquely describes me as the "Pest of the Permanent Staff." Tenderly asked me why I hated drill... How can I tell her that the sight of so many women strutting up and down repels me?

August 21st

A letter to dear, foolish Michael. I wish someone would write to me. Had devilish job borrowing half-crown: bunged off birthday 'grams to Hag No. 1 and Donald (of Magdalen) whose birthdays were yesterday or the day before.

August 22nd

Ho! Ho!! To tea at Baldock mansions! Liked Richard's ma immensely – rather vague and very untidy. Richard desperately trying to teach me the mysterious game of chess. Rupert driving everyone mad by thumping monotonously on the piano and chanting unrecognisable songs.

August 23rd

Rupert frantically mowing the overgrown tennis-court: Richard chasing me (sun-suit: sweater: bare legs) around the summer-house. Lazily knocked a few balls around the court: returned to "Melbourne House" for a meal. Rupert's teaching a very stupid me, the finer art of poker.

August 24th

Painful sojourn at the dentist's. Have enough metal to make three tanks, now. Found my dear, soulful Richard guzzling beer at the "Crown": swept him off to see a reputedly funny film. Beautiful night – moon thinly veiled by faint clouds: trees overhead: river flowing peacefully. "Dear God, the very houses seem asleep. . . "

August 25th

Delightfully unexpected letter from a Navy man who has just returned from Malta. Apparently he's written at the instigation of dear Aubrey Hart: they're "great pals." He urges me to write MORE and OFTEN. I will....!! Didn't think AH cared a damn about letters.

August 26th

Darling Michael again: assures me that he loves me much too much to argue indefinitely – this is in reply to my beastly letter last April. I wonder if I meant it when I wrote back today and said "wherever I go, whoever I meet, I shall never lose one little ambition – to own six white-headed brats with mechanical minds."

August 27th

Ha! Kathleen has not deserted me. Now at Skegness, Lincs. Quite happy – thank heaven. Dentist gaily yanked a tooth out. Frightfully tight on whiskey - and - cider – Effie's binge. Heard terribly funny yarns about her grandmother who was on the stage: wore tights: sang songs like "Champagne Charlie". Marion, Effie and I decided to swim in the river at 11.30pm., but I was sick out of the window.

August 28th

Flannelfoot munter most perturbed by my performance last night : I told her that I was very pleased and that I'd made a very neat job of it. I also reproached her for her language: this is known as counter-attack. Very hot day: played tennis with Richard in the cool evening. Letter from Gillian.

August 29th

Desperately seeking excuses to get out in the sunshine. Teaming with Shropshire rain tonight. Concentrated on letter-writing – produced two commendable efforts – 12 pages to Johnnie; 12 to Kathleen; airgraph to Scranny B.

August 30th

It rains – and how it rains. Richard's mother gave me a piece of cake. Fed and boozed with Marion and May. A dreadful little airman insisted on taking me back to camp; rather perturbed by my mournful wailings of "I want Richard!!"

August 31st

Bags of panic: lots of tiring rows with this objectional new cove: the ghastly two-taped specimen in charge of the disorderly room. Almost landed on a charge, but talked my way out of it.

1942			SEPTEMBER			1942
M	T	W	T	F	S	S
..	1	2	3	4	5	6
7	8	9	10	11	12	13
14	15	16	17	18	19	20
21	22	23	24	25	26	27
28	29	30	..	..	..	..

September 1st

Bags of lovely letters – from the Mater who's very depressed; from Donald of Magdalen – as irresponsible as ever; and from Buddy, who's also sent me his song "My wonderful dream's come true." He has dedicated it to me – and also accuses me of being its inspiration!

September 2nd

Rumours are winging their way around! Such rumours – we are moving – to Morecambe, to Gloucester; to Hereford; to "ops" station. I shall maintain a dignified silence – or perhaps it would be fun to start a few rumours off my own back!

September 3rd

Bunged in an application for leave: must get away from chattering, screaming, rumour-mongering women for a few days. With the blasé Bee, the buxom Peggy and the rustic Winsome, saw an 'Ensa' production of Noel Coward's "Private Lives."

September 4th

"Here I am on charge again! On a little 252[1] again...." – new version of a popular song! In trouble again – this time at the special request of their worships – Technical Training Command. As far as I can gather, it's something connected with wasting paper – ho! Ho! Richard drinking a lot and then declaring passionate and everlasting love for his little mare.

September 5th

My charge seems to have faded into oblivion! Hasn't spoiled my appetite! May and I demolished eggs on toast, chocolate cakes and gallons of tea. Saw the film version of Shaw's "Major Barbara"; loved some of the lines. Half-a-pint – and then some more food. Returned to the inevitable "Crown" and talked to Bob who's very attractive and likes to imagine that he's a Communist. Minor upheaval with friend Richard.

---

[1] RAF Form No. 252 – For recording breaches of discipline:

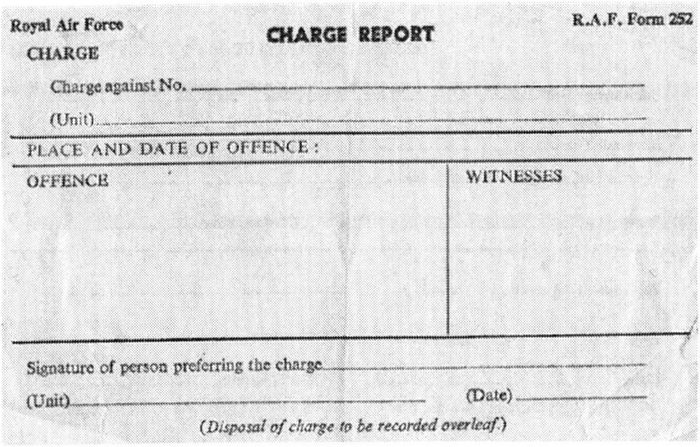

Royal Air Force

R.A.F. Form 252

CHARGE REPORT

CHARGE

Charge against No. ....

(Unit) ....

PLACE AND DATE OF OFFENCE :

OFFENCE	WITNESSES

Signature of person preferring the charge ....

(Unit) .... (Date) ....

(Disposal of charge to be recorded overleaf.)

September 7th

What a waste of emotion – didn't go to the concert after all – 'bus queue too long. Went to a film and laughed a lot. Felt a Woman To Be Admired in my ancient frock, my still-presentable stockings and high heels. Felt rather high on only four beers. Rupert strumming on the piano until midnight; Richard almost uncontrollable. Richard persuaded me to undress in the bathroom (dangerous practice!) and then ruthlessly attacked me! His ma discovered us in a passionate embrace on the veranda, but was very reasonable.

September 8th

Spent the morning practising R's expressions of guilt when R's mother looked my way, but – good scout – she said nothing. The burg looked sleepily peaceful in the sunshine this morning, and I felt glad that Richard persuaded me to stay. My Dorset instinct is as strong as ever but lorry-riding on hot days is so uncomfortable. Took the boat up the river and swam; I prefer the sea to the Severn. Phoned Marion; heard there was a wire from Buddy – something very obscure about meeting him in Sussex. Bunged one back about "unforeseen complications."

September 9th

Woke with a clear conscience this morning. Changed a castle and a pawn when R. was out, and – beat him! He was suspicious and I confessed. I have a sinister suspicion that I'm very fond of Richard – it seems absurd 21 and 17!! Found a letter from bro' George. He adds a "touching PS" – (I) Don't get married. (II) Don't get engaged!!!!???

September 10th

Pleasant evening at Beryl's billet[1]. One eye on her magazines and one on the clock. Just departing – hoping to dash up to High Town – when her billeter brought sandwiches and coffee.

September 11th

Duty – always duty!! Accomplished an airgraph to George H. Griffin, a/Pantryman and started to wrestle with a complicated screed to "Nickie" (who has complained of my apparent neglect) when the 'phone rang. It was my beloved Shropshire Lad – checking on my alibi – methinks!

September 12th

Fearfully late for tea at "Melbourne House." Van Vean (let's-all-be-girls-together) made matters worse by stopping me in the town for a little chew-up. I cut short the confab. by saying that I had absolutely no conscience as far as the service was concerned. With Richard, saw a film – one that ended with a spot of flags-flying – trumpets – blowing- we're-the-unbeatable-British-type of poetry.

September 13th

Heavenly afternoon – wonderful wangle! Wore a sweater with collar-and-tie, underneath my tunic and shorts 'neath my skirt. Waited impatiently until we reached a more deserted part of the river and then did a very refined sort of strip-tease. Richard trusted me with the rowing – but only in the widest and loneliest part. Presented Mrs. B. with one of Jane's kittens.

---

[1] A place, especially a civilian's house, where soldiers are lodged temporarily; more colloquially any place to stop or stay.

September 14th

Not a damn' letter from anyone. Oh hell! What's happened to my so-called friends? Richard and I saw "Tatter's Castle" – a truly superb film. Met Madge and Peggy, Marion, May and Winsome. Richard bought some rum and I drank Madge's, too. I felt very sleepy and rather amorous.

September 16th

Completely haywire letter from the glamorous Yvonne. Going to town with her boss to produce some shows. Sent a morbid letter to Johnnie.

September 18th

Scrawled note from Gillian N. – and a photo. Poor dear's haring off to Loughborough[1] – Oct 4 – ho! Going to be an instructor!! Also a letter from Gretta; dashed off an incoherent reply, as she's feeling lonely. Got very bored with an inevitable farewell binge. Felt like weeping with joy when Richard loomed up on the bleared horizon.

September 19th

Very sad day: arrived too late for Madge's wedding – the ceremony and the reception. Peggy and I guzzled the remains and I spent the evening climbing in and out of the gown and gazing at the enchanted reflection of me in a bridal veil. A squint-eyed woman thumping on the piano made me feel very morbid.

---

[1] RAF Loughborough – WAAF Officer's School (1941-42)

September 20th

Filthily cold: pouring with rain. Manchester whole-heartedly living up to its reputash[1]. , depressing train journey - nothing to read. Consoled myself by being very rude to Chris Lumsden, whom I dislike intensely.

September 21st

Say nuffink ! Say nuffink! "Out of the frying pan..." I'm going to No. 2 WAAF. Depot[2] but it's at Gloucester - quite convenient for a southern maid. Sent an airgraph to Michael.

September 22nd

Beryl stood me tea at the "Cavalier". Letter from Kay who has tonsillitis, sent me "Lilliput." Bright epistle from Effie - now with HQ. Naval Intelligence at Liverpool. Heard some Handel - "Fireworks" music, Chess rapidly improving - Richard spent three hours thinking hard before he finally beat me.

---

[1] "Reputash.": short for reputation.

[2] RAF Innsworth, to the north of Gloucester housed No. 2 WAAF Depot from December 1941 and retained a training role throughout WWII.

September 23rd

Good excuse to avoid the wing party – Beethoven's Fifth being broadcast. Very disturbed emotionally: wept. Richard still panicking about the difference in our ages. Arrived towards the end of the farewell affair: Joe from Accounts snaffled some sandwiches for me. Adjutant delightfully democratic (!). Marion says that she's been tenderly enquiring about my absence the whole evening. Also said "Griffin thinks I'm a fool." M. brightly reassured her that I did!

September 24th

Two letters from Johnnie – rather dull.

September 25th

Kidnapped by Marion and old Joe Beach, persuaded by brute force to drink beer and rum and pep with them. A rather slewed me finally escaped at 9.30 pm, staggered along to "Melbourne House" and drank tea and made very bright conversation.

September 26th

Tea with Beryl: quiet evening at the B's – usual game of chess – usual result: Richard won.

September 27th

Last night in Shropshire. Strangely enough, did no drinking. Lost at chess: lost at Monopoly – but who could expect to win, playing with the notorious Baldock bros? Richard has threatened to haunt me. Feel quite happy and not at all sentimental.

September 28th

Frantic two hours trying to cram everything into my kit bag. Fruitless. Damn' awful train journey with hordes of screaming women, panicking about their luggage. Peggy improved matters by insisting on my nursing her kitten - most uncomfortable. High spot - row with a flight Sergt just after arriving.

September 29th

Maggie Bond and I are living together but she's working with some of the old Bridgnorth gang and I've been shoved into a room of strange women. Feel rather miserable. Joyce and Peggy are in another part of the camp. Friendly gathering of familiar faces in the YMCA. All discussed "Good old Bridgnorth" in fearfully loud voices: cheered me somewhat.

September 30th

The people with whom I work are too, too polite. They make me sick. They're very conscientious and oh! So promotion-keen! Oh for Bridgnorth and the noise and the cussing and the rude remarks and the good-natured banters. I feel like a fish out of water. Writing scores of letters - in the hope that people will reply soon, and lighten my misery.

1942			OCTOBER			1942
M	T	W	T	F	S	S
..	..	..	1	2	3	4
5	6	7	8	9	10	11
12	13	14	15	16	17	18
19	20	21	22	23	24	25
26	27	28	29	30	31	..

October 1st

Hilarious epistle from Kathleen – the Groupie is sending her to Air Ministry for a commish. board. She wants my opinion on the matter. Huh! She should know! Airgraph from Ronald Y., (Fleet Air Arm) now training in Canada. Hopefully addressed "Corporal D. Griffin." Cheerfully assumes that I know that Kemp is buried in Hamburg. Felt depressed – very keen on Kemp in my 'teens.

October 2nd

Three rip-roaring cheers for America – Buddy has written a very mournful letter, in which he says he's disgusted with everything. Postal system's b-y – letter's taking ten days to arrive. Sent me a Tolstoy poem – translated of course. Ah! Life has its brighter moments.

October 3rd

Such a lovely letter from my "loving and ever-faithful Richard" (his own words). I am very, very fond of him. Spent the afternoon in Gloucester with Dorothy H. and Margaret B. Rather tame but very peaceful and quite pleasant. Saw a film which made my public-house laugh ring out many times.

October 4th

Another day of exploration – this time Cheltenham. Teeming with Yanks – none compares with Buddy. Good meal and olde, olde film.

October 5th

I still feel bored to tears with the incredible orderly room – and personnel. Mournfully meander around, cursing quietly. Rapidly bringing my correspondence up-to-date: writing stacks of scatty epistles.

October 6th

'Nother letter from my "still loving, and even more faithful Richard." Saw a very funny film at the camp "Ritz-Plaza." Occupied my usual conspicuous position – front row.

October 7th

Rather sad letter from Joan: her sweet father's dead. Joan flown home in bomber for funeral. Letter from the mater – enclosing two from Johnnie who's arrived in India. Envelopes plastered with intriguing stamps. He's much amused by India – he says it's not at all glamorous.

October 8th

Odd little Czech woman who sleeps opposite spends her odd moments trying to explain her matrimonial tangle to me. Good thing I'm a calm and sympathetic type (who'd believe me?)

October 9th

Usual dull day. Kept an eagle-eyed – but unsuccessful watch on the mail. No more letters. I think I shall send some very rude cables to Malta, the Middle East and the Transvaal – just to shake my inattentive former lovers.

October 10th

'gram from Beryl who's arriving on Monday. Also, another sweet letter from my dear Richard.

October 11th

Bankrupt as usual, so stuck down my name for a party at the Yank camp. A rather boring specimen from Nawth Carolahna (!) tagged along, but I managed to escape at intervals and join Peggy and her rowdy gang in a hectic version of "broken bottles." Returned to camp at 1 o'clock with one can of American beer.

October 12th

Foul after-taste of beer and peanuts – most memorable thing today.

October 13th

Such a peculiar letter from Buddy. Being a particularly intelligent specimen, I've read between the lines and assume that he's going overseas. Feel depressed – only temporarily, I hope. I should like to see him – despite this irresistible spell cast by my beloved Shropshire lad.

October 14th

Bunged off masses of sheets covered in my almost illegible scrawl, to Richard of Shropshire. I feel vaguely happy about my pending flying visit to Bridgnorth.

October 15th

Ah ha! Hip – hip – hurrah day. Joyfully collected two pounds and six bob from my friend, the Accountant man, and after gaily marching away, bumped into that morbid commish – wallah, Beryl, H-B., bemoaning her fate. Sent an air-mail letter to Johnnie – expect reply, six months.

October 16th

Two letters from Gillian Nicholson – who's fed to the teeth at Loughborough. Also a cheerful epistle from Marion R., who's beating up at Bishopbriggs[1]. Rolled into camp flicks with Peggy and saw the remains of a funny film – usual matrimonial tangle.

---

[1] A Scottish town just north of Glasgow. Home during WWII to RAF Bishopbriggs, No. 18 Balloon Centre, also used as a transit camp when being posted between the south of England and the north of Scotland.

October 17th

Blithely sailed out of camp at lunch-time. Rode in a lorry through the wonderful golden-red countryside. Arrived in Bridgnorth in style – American Army car. Pleasant feeling of quiet happiness at Melbourne House. Drank three beers with the brothers: spent a virtuous night – no verandah escapades.

October 18th

Pleasant morning with the dog while Mrs. B. and Richard were at church and Rupert gadding around with the Home Guard. Dear Cecilia gracing the house with her presence later. Richard becoming very difficult – only able to control him by throwing the chess board etc. into the air. Uncomfortable return journey in lorries – walked miles, too: half-an-hour late. Huh!

October 19th

That man Michael's here again – two letters and some happy photos. He hints at a letter – a very serious letter – he's about to write. I suppose it's a confession of some hectic affair he's had in the desert. Oh dear! He still hopes that I shall be waiting when he returns. Which reminds me – heard from Effie who's getting in some good work on behalf of the Great Venture – wrangling introductions with the right people in Liverpool.

October 20th

Letter from the love-stricken Richard. Sent an airgraph winging its way to the Middle East – to Michael; and an air mail letter, too. Ah! Poor puzzled little Squiff!

October 21st

My ex-lovers – now overseas – are here again – Scranny, with a completely haywire poem, and an air mail letter from Aubrey (Malta)

October 22nd

Airgraph from Johnnie. Poor dear hasn't received any mail and to improve matters – it rains in India, too.

October 23rd

Still frantically trying to cope with my mail: wrote to Gillian and Yvonne. Hared over to Cheltenham with Peggy to see a film. The exorbitant admission price (2/6) almost spoiled my enjoyment; however, it was in technicolour.

October 25th

Teeming with rain: crouched over the fire: thumped out an occasional stupid letter on the typewriter just to pacify the damned silly adjutant. Smoked an enormous number of fags[1] and went to the camp flicks with Peggy.

---

[1] Slang term for cigarettes

October 26th

Hitched to Oxford with Beryl – my first visit for eight months. Delighted to find Laurie and Carpie still at the "Kettle", also saw Donald B., - whom I last met in June, '41. He's still busy – failing exams. Swept B. and me along to his rooms in Holywell Street: played all the records that I used to love – Chopin; Wagner; Beethoven. Sentimental Squiffy wanted to weep. B. and I rode in a lorry; arrived in Cheltenham absolutely drenched – but wildly happy.

October 27th

The hopeless Richard was in Oxford yesterday. I did so much want to see him, but – perhaps Fate foresaw the complications that would've arisen: Donald enthusiastically describing my wild days – and nights – in Oxford; and Richard being difficult.

October 28th

Rumours that Mrs. Roosevelt is visiting the depot soon- thank God I shan't be here. "The pomp and vanity" – and the emptiness and futility of it! Stupid waste of time!

October 29th

Letter from the "still love-stricken R." Accounts people generously presented me with three guineas – cheering thought. Stuffed all sorts of unwanted odds and ends in an awful old case (ex-Beryl's) and paddled thro' the usual downpour to the 'bus stop. Ghastly journey: felt a wreck. Arrived home at midnight and tackled a meal (incl. cheese): no time for conversation. Found two letters – one from Gillian who suggests some complicated plan for a meeting. Other was from an old flame – David A. who's marooned in Cornwall – training to be a pilot: rather amazing – his popping up again after 2 years.

October 30th

What does this morning bring? A heavy head, two cats on my bed – egg and tomato for breakfast and airgraph from Johnnie – in hospital. Wonder what he's doing there? Lounged around in red sweater, the historic slacks and even more ancient suede shoes. Bohemian – but comfortable – and no-one to yell – 'Hair off your collar, Griffin!'

October 31st

Walked to the beach: was introduced to a weird woman who'd been married four times. Definitely a type – but quite amusing. Letter from Georgie Hubert – posted in New York in Sept. Complains of a "shaky head." Ha. According to the radio, he's been to Russia since then.

1942			NOVEMBER			1942
M	T	W	T	F	S	S
..	..	..	..	..	..	1
2	3	4	5	6	7	8
9	10	11	12	13	14	15
16	17	18	19	20	21	22
23/30	24	25	26	27	28	29

November 1st

Beethoven's happy 8th Symphony. Lazy day. Wrote to Richard: airgraphs to Young (Canada) and one to Georgie Hubert.

November 2nd

Saw "Fantasia" – third time. I still disagree with Disney's representation of Beethoven's 4th. However!...

November 3rd

Sat in the second-front row of the Regent and sulked the whole way through the third-rate and incredibly dull film. Called in to see cousin's offspring – peculiar looking child, just like a goldfish. Controlled my thoughts: remembered to say the right things.

November 4th

The Battle of Egypt seems to haunt me – the radio blares it; the headlines scream at me; people discuss it. And my heart says – "and what of Michael?" Oh Michael! For God's sake cable me or something.

November 5th

Usual awful rush of last-minute packing: just managed to leap into the super-special Somerset-Dorset train. Buried myself in a morbid book called "After the verdict." The author frequently quoted "they are not long, the weeping and the laughter, I think they have no portion in us after, we pass the Gates." The words throbbed in my mind as I stared through the windows.

November 6th

This place seems so strange… I still feel an outsider, and – yet, everyone is so charming – someone had made my bed and warmed my slippers, last night. I wish it was over and done with – and I could climb out of my uniform for the last time. I found a reams long letter from Richard last night. Found I've left my damned identity card at home: managed to get out of camp – and back – with Maggie B's – who doesn't resemble me in the slightest. Saw "This was Paris" with Peggy.

November 7th

I work and work – so hard and so long: no mail. Began a dull letter to Richard, but went to bed after the first page.

November 8th

Today, I work again, and swear a lot and scowl at the hateful typewriter. I eat too much and feel sick.

November 9th

Note from Mrs G. – with my 1250[1]. Long epistle in the neat handwriting of Marion Rogers. She's met an airman who knew me in my hectic youth. Beryl and I hared off to Cheltenham to celebrate her 21st. Had quite a good dinner in a very respectable and very-Cheltenham hotel with the paint peeling off the dining-room walls: didn't interfere with my appetite, though. Later adjourned to the dilapidated "Dogtail" Bar where we drank gin-and-it and made an insufficient lager last for half an hour. Third-rate Yanks and some dagoish civilians eyed us as possible victims so we disgustedly grabbed our greatcoats and hopped on the bus.

November 10th

Peggy and I saw an extremely entertaining film – "The man who came to dinner". Beryl presented me with Peter Fleming's "One's Company" – this time it's a tale of China. The thought that I can read it only in odd minutes is infuriating: I'd like to settle down and lose myself for hours at a stretch in his lazy – and yet vivid – descriptions of that fascinating country. Charming letter from Mrs. B – delightful person.

---

[1] RAF ID Card – Form 1250 or F1250.

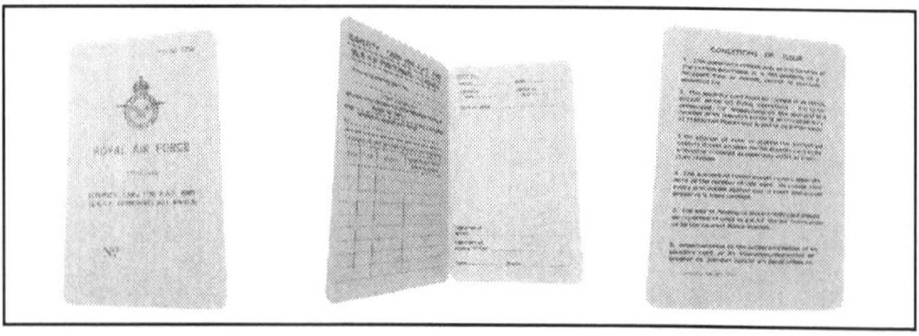

November 11th

Letter from Tony (ex Magdalen) who's about to become a very dashing sec. Loot in the R.A., and who wants me to meet him in Town next month. Haven't a rag to wear but I think I'll speak to Beryl, who has a lovely black suit, a six-guinea hat and some Dutch boy shoes. I wonder if black will suit me...

November 14th

A rather dull letter from Scatty. G. with the bankrupt Peggy, thumbed lorries and cars and reached the ever-depressing Kidderminster in time for a very large meal. Found my ever-lovable Richard in his favourite chair with his pipe and a welcoming smile. Spent an hour in the "Squirrel" where a wise - but wicked old local bought us beer, we retaliated with whiskey - which brought forth some old songs - and an invitation to supper. Looked at faded photos of the Boer war thru a bleary haze and munched bread and cheese. Returned to Melbourne House at midnight; found Mrs. B. cheerfully meandering around with sheets and things: tumultuous splashing noise from the bathroom - Peggy invited for the night. So much for my blissful dreams of a peaceful weekend....

November 15th

Relaxed with "One's Company" while Peggy took Bobs up to camp and everybody else went to church! Bells pealing this morning – wonderful to hear them; heralding peace to come.... I wonder? I hope! Richard moody because I threw him out of my room last night. Little Squiff just as difficult – for the same reason. He – unsatisfied; I – frustrated. So sad ... Mollie as charming as ever (ha!) Peggy and I reluctantly left at teatime. Made the return journey in speedy lorries: arrived back in time for a cup of tea at the YMCA. And a spot of hymn – singing with a padre hammering on the piano and another exercising his lungs with "Abide With Me" – Gran Poore's favourite hymn.

November 16th

Accomplished a difficult letter to Mrs. B. – and an even more difficult one to her precious son (my honest opinion). I feel sick and fed to the teeth with this racket. Now amusing myself by planning unofficial weekends – feel really desperate.

November 17th

Gave my inside the time of its life tonight – loaded it with peanuts, canned beer and spam sandwiches, and then gave the whole mixture a good shaking up by jitterbugging around with a hot-footed Yank. I laughed a lot; in fact, it was quite an enjoyable evening, but I met no-one worth "dating". Still – it was fun – even tho' my stomach punished me.

November 18th

Letter from Mrs. G. who b-y well makes me sick sometimes; fond of her though I am. She's panicking like hell about some damn' silly piece of paper which was attached to the clothes coupons that the old man gave me – and which I passed to her, as I haven't any money anyway.

November 19th

I feel more than a little happy – I've had a letter from Fishface, written in August. Left New York in September (letter I mean) and has spent some time wandering around Shropshire and this b-y place. Says a little about his romances, and generously imparts a smattering of his philosophy as far as love affairs are concerned. Apparently he's just discovered that it's more fun – and far safer to be in love with several people instead on the conventional one-and-only.

November 20th

Found a new way to pass the dreary day – I load coal on the fire, which infuriates the temperamental grate so it retaliates by allowing the front to fall in. And so I struggle on – much to the amusement of a gang of feeble, scruffy women who appear to be permanent fixtures – no-one has yet discovered who they are or what their vital war job is.

November 21st

I have stomach-ache (due to the so-called wonderful system of Nature – huh!) and I detest the typewriter that I'm compelled to use. I entered the hut at lunchtime, and – my heart sank – no letters on my bed. I was working myself into a weep when – someone came with a letter from Richard – how I love him. If I do not remain faithful it will be the fault of some powerful force behind me because I am now and forever more very fond of him. I wish he'd dare to rape me – and then force me to marry him.

November 22nd

Such a long day: P. and I, after an afternoon spent scrounging, had sufficient for ten fags and two front seats at the camp cinema. Good sixpennoth, too. Nazis mixed up in the film, as usual.

November 25th

Huge scrawl of Beryl H-B looms up on my narrow horizon. She describes the fighter station as a "b-y dive" – probably means that she's about to have fun.

November 26th

Decided to have the afternoon off. P. and I whizzed into Cheltenham in a Yank truck: the driver gave us some genuine chewing gum. Feverish hunt for lipstick: a foul old woman persuaded me to buy some putrid stuff which she swore was dark red; transpired to be a beastly orange. Ferociously scowled at the Polyphoto[1] woman; results should be really frightening.

November 27th

Saw an amusing film at the camp flicks – or did I? No, I think it was another night: I can't remember.

November 28th

Card from Gillian – who's wangled herself to Devonshire. She threatens a letter in the near future. Set off at lunchtime, armed with Stella Gibbons' "Cold Comfort Farm". So engrossed that when darkness fell I was stranded outside Chippenham. Wept with temper until a bus stopped. Later, furtively crawled aboard a much-despised train. Gorged fish cake and chips at Salisbury at midnight and chatted with a Scots soldier (not the kilted type) whose aunt's an undertaker. At 2.30am saw the moon light on the sea at Whitecliff – home again – and glad to be home. Found a letter from Scranny Baker and a card from Aubrey – very simple but typical of Malta.

---

[1] Polyfoto: A special camera made by Kodak took 48 pictures in quick succession onto a glass plate negative offering up to 48 poses delivered back as a 48 photo proof sheet from which enlargements could be selected. Polyfoto concession booths were operated in major cities.

November 29th

Deserved to stay in bed until early afternoon so – I did. Dug out a very old tweed suit and went to the local flicks. Leonard confides that he thinks I'll grow up to be an old maid…! Out of the mouths of babes, etc.

November 30th

Mother so insistent on my returning by train (so safe) that I marched into the booking office and bought a shilling ticket right under her aristocratic nose without her even suspecting that foul play was afoot! Hopped out at Blandford and hailed a lorry. Driver forced the old thing to do 60 mph while I feverishly gnawed an apple and prepared my soul for an untimely end. Reached camp safely and punctually – to my eternal surprise.

1942		DECEMBER				1942
M	T	W	T	F	S	S
..	1	2	3	4	5	6
7	8	9	10	11	12	13
14	15	16	17	18	19	20
21	22	23	24	25	26	27
28	29	30	31	..	..	..

December 1st

Letters from Richard (who appears to spend his time taking Bobs for walks) and from May Henderson, now in Bedfordshire. Richard accuses my letters of causing "a cheerful glow" to emanate from him. He also says "I get an overwhelmingly detached frame of mind when I see you wrestling with the House at Pooh Corner" Ha! The great Griffin intellect wrestling with AA Milne! I read the C.R. books for their very simplicity.

December 2nd

I've been reading Alan Baker's letter. His opinion "I hate the thought of you being unhappily married. You were meant for happiness & laughter & sentimental tears and the joy mixed with pain that music & poetry can give, and real physical love." I wonder – shall I ever find it?

December 5th

Beryl's gotten herself involved with a S/Ldr who is 36 but looks 50. Damn the woman. She gaily writes a lot of tripe about little black pills. I'll screw her ears off when I see her. Spent a pleasant afternoon in Glos with Maggie B and Dorothy H. Saw an Abbot & Costello film – almost had hysterics. Sent cables to Johnnie & Aubrey; the others have to be content with airgraphs.

December 6th

Gillian has seen the man who knows the man – not about a posting but about my watch keeping. Oh! Echo of the wonderful past when I dreamed dreams and had visions of ops. Rooms. I refuse to believe in or to hope that everything will really happen – but I feel that life & the future has suddenly became so much brighter.

December 19th

Hared off to London with P. S. Rode in Yank jeeps and a speedy yank staff car (complete with dashing American officer and the nephew of the famous Sgt. York[1]) Visit to Oxford delayed our arrival in town by 3 hours. Effie 8 hours late. Drank gin in the "Cole Hole" and the foul stinking-of-cats "Bunch of Grapes". Headed for Peggy's house at a very late hour: climbed through the window, made tea and went to bed at 3 am.

[1] Sergeant York was a decorated soldier of WWI, and a 1941 film with Gary Cooper.

December 20th

Much preparation for breakfast: Effie racing around South London on a bike; Peggy exploring the pantry: these expeditions produced fresh bread rolls and – ah! Heinz baked beans. Over breakfast Effie & I enthusiastically discussing round the world trip. Hitched across London and eventually abandoned the irritable Effie somewhere between Watford & Aylesbury. Late meal at the G.K. (Oxford) and later drank much beer with two yanks who came speeding out of the darkness in a very large lorry.

December 21st

I thought I was imagining things (due to my pitiable condish) when I read Fishface's (South Africa) letter last night, but no! it reads just the same this morning: he has collected 15 pairs of silk stockings for me. I shall indulge in a super attach of blood pressure when he returns.

December 22nd

Christmas cards rolling in from all the old boozers. Whacking parcel from my mother – dear person. Also a reasonable amount of ever welcome cash.

December 25th

Arose at an early hour and mechanically & meaninglessly wished everybody "A Happy Christmas". Ha! Ate a huge lunch: NAAFI. Beer inspired me to type airgraphs to all the beloved in the far-flung outposts. Richard phoned. Went to Camp flicks. Odd sort of Christmas.

December 26th

Meandered along the road to Worcester until I was picked up by a bad tempered lorry driver. He apparently wasn't very fond of WAAFs. Felt overjoyed at the sight of Richard who – persuasive devil – talked me into returning to Melbourne House with him. At long last met the eccentric aunt Cecil, who tries to be very frightening but fails, rather.

December 27th

Peeled apples under Aunt C's critical eye, while everybody else went to church. A pleasant day: I refused to be either disturbed or impressed by Aunt C's rather pointed talk on the Church of England (the old dear ran a mission school in Jamaica in her wild youth). Rode on a lorry to Worcester: plenty of time but I spoiled things by getting on a train going the wrong way. Eventually reached this "other Eden" at 2 am on Monday.

December 28th

Not sufficient punishment to wake up feeling damn tired. Oh no! I have to go on charge to satisfy those with a lust for red tape. The judge made some very nasty remarks but I emerged unscathed - surprised me somewhat. Had disturbing visions (that's not the right word) of little Squif becoming a punker-Walla for a few days. A change would be welcome, anyway.

December 30th

Heigh Ho!! For bonny Scotland. Rode in the Guards van to Birmingham and there joined in the marathon for the Scots train. Absolutely crammed to overflowing. The class conscious railway people had locked the first class carriage but undaunted hoards of people in uniform climbed in: someone heaved me from behind and I went sailing over the heads of those already in. I helped to haul middle aged biz. men in – fun & games, what ho! Squatted in the corridor and tried to listen to one of the M-A.B.M. very knowledgeably talking about insects & life in Malaya. I bore it as I'd spotted his flask: he shared his tea and spam sandwiches with me but spoiled his generous gesture by trying to make love to me. With a gay laugh and a shrug of the shoulders, I launched into a discussion on "Young men I have loved" – only means of escape.

December 31st

Marion on tip toe at Glasgow station – complete with Canadian boyfriend. Spent a busy 2 hours criticising Bishopsbriggs & Innsworth and reminiscing on "good old Bridgnorth". Reached May's house in time for a wacking lunch. In the evening, honoured the village 'hop' with our gracious presence. I jiggered around with a 15 year old local black sheep - quite well behaved on this auspicious occasion. The good whiskey at May's house was very effective and I fell asleep. Everyone accused me of "passing out". Most unkind. Odd males drift in and out, sampling the whiskey in between entry and exit, and several people, with and more frequently – without voices, sang but none surpassed the flirtatious Marion's rather beautiful rendering of "Over the sea to Skye". I was semi conscious most of the time, and I ached for a soft bed and deep sleep – which I didn't have until 4 am.

1943			JANUARY			1943
M	T	W	T	F	S	S
..	..	..	..	1	2	3
4	5	6	7	8	9	10
11	12	13	14	15	16	17
18	19	20	21	22	23	24
25	26	27	28	29	30	31

January 1st

The day passed quickly – I slept until sunset. May & Marion spent the day haring over the countryside with their last night's sleeping partners. Another village hop tonight so – the three blind mice went. I found myself jiggering around with the village black sheep again when – suddenly and without warning 6'2" of Naval loot walked in and murmuring "of course you dance", swept me into a waltz to the distorted rendering of "Love is all, love is all – it's the cause of it all. . ." Helped Miles (the Navy) and some Army loots[1] (very Grenadierish and oh so Guardish!) to demolish a bottle of whiskey and then return to Nether Place – the G.G. mess, where I had a little gin, was violently sick, and decided to stay the night.

(Cont'd)

[1] Loots or loot: Lieutenant

The Navy forced mustard and water down my protesting throat: the G.G. filed in odd shades of pyjamas tenderly enquiring "How are you, darling?" The Navy, meanwhile, rushed in and out bemoaning the loss of his green pyjamas (they didn't fit me very well, anyway) and I felt so sorry for him that I was forced to say "For God's sake, sleep with me and shut up." He tried to seduce me but wasn't successful – approach utterly wrong.

January 2nd

Tea in bed – served by the fair hand of Lt David Ferguson, GG. He's very sweet, comes from Hampshire, knows Michael's step sister and has an enquiring eyebrow… specially the morning after such a night. Feeling very fresh and rather gay, walked back to "Glenlussa"[1] where everyone was still slumbering. Nine o'clock chimed as I crept upstairs in stockinged feet. There was yet another dance tonight so, after bidding au revoir to Marion (going out for a spot of fresh air (in the boiler house) with a Grenadier Guard in tow, May & I made a bee line for David & Quinnie (very dull young man who goes to bed early) Quinnie obviously a hopeless case so May & I bet 5 bob on David making passionate love to one of us. Enticed him back to Glenlussa, when I changed in slacks and a sweater, and won round one: May unfairly inveigled him into a bedroom on the pretext of showing him to the bathroom. However, I spoiled her charming little game by whizzing into the bedroom, squatting on the floor and loudly commenting on the enchanting scene. David deserted May and attacked me – this fact the fair May denies. M.H. most annoyed so we tactfully handed D his hat and wished him "goodnight" – and what a good night.

---

[1] Research suggests "Glenlussa" was a private house rather than the place on the Kintyre peninsula.

January 3rd

Leisurely cruised over to Catteran[1] where some very hospitable people (parents of one of May's lovers) gave us a very good meal. Passed a pleasant evening giggling at some idiotic Charlie Chaplin films. Returned to "Glenlussa" at midnight to hear that there had been 3 phone calls for "the Duchess of Dorset"; "Miss Squiffy Griffy", etc, could gnash my teeth with frustration!

January 4th

Met my Friday night sleeping partner on the station this morning. Frigidly eyed one another and politely said "Good morning", he looked as dashing as only a naval lieutenant can look. Saw him again at Glasgow: the wenches bet me five bob that I wouldn't wish him "good torpedo aiming". He spoiled the game by strolling up to me: friendly goodbyes and amused glances at one another. I had great difficulty in keeping my face reasonable straight. Spent the afternoon with a bottle of whiskey belonging to M. Rogers and 12 bottles of beer belonging to Dan (the Canadian) at Marion's house. No one to make love to, so sent long and incoherent telegrams to the Mater and to Richard. In bed with May, amused myself by composing my own obscene (only vaguely, though) version of "Thanks for the memory...of nights in Nether Place".

---

[1] There remains a question of if Catteran was a real place; perhaps the place name was miss-heard in a Scottish accent by Dorothy and there were no road signs in war-time to allow her to crib a correct spelling for the diary?

January 5th

I rose very late: breakfast cooked by Marion – very good too. Called on some relations of May's who live in a very exclusive part of Glasgow. Fun & games at the station: spent the late evening wondering around Mauchline – me hoping to see David: May & Marion hoping for any old thing. Whiskey at the Poosie Nansie's beforehand. – effects soon – too soon – wore off, and I felt very forsaken. May & Marion gaily careering around with two Grenadier Guardsmen. I feel most dissatisfied with fate – or whoever guides my destiny.

January 6th

Stayed in bed until lunch time: then went down in pyjamas. Remained in this slovenly state until a longing for cigarettes drove the two besoms to nagging me into cycling into town. It was rather fun – steering the bikes through the banks of slush: trying to prevent the flapping legs of my pants from becoming entangled with the chain. Sight of a telephone too much, hopped off and phoned Grenadier Guard place. Reluctant soldier at other end grudgingly promised to give David a message. Three hours later, David called me: urged me to tear down to the Loudoun Arms – time very limited. About to depart in a cloud of dust – or perhaps snow would be more appropriate – when phone rang again – the two besoms to say that David had been sighted. Said something very rude and very appropriate. Found David and two others looking very businesslike in battledress complete with walking sticks and flasks of rum – yum! Yum! Why must they have manoeuvres on my last night here?

January 7th

Slid down the road to the station, persuaded May to make me a present of 20 fags and bade her farewell. Arrived in Glasgow to hear that the train had left half an hour earlier. Marion & I drift around various shops and I collected a burgundy lipstick, some tobacco (to appease my father), something for K and something for May's mother. Left at one p.m., hung out of the window, screaming reassurances at Marion regarding a good old binge in town in the near future. Eleven hours later arrived at Gloucester – gloomy hole.

January 9th

Buddy here again – or rather a long letter from North Africa. I thought that was where he'd gone: so pleased that I'd guessed right. He says nothing about N.A., because he says "I want my letters to you be different from the other letters that I write". He also rather unmistakably hinted at his particular reason for wanting the war to finish. What's to be become of me? (Shades of Shaw's Eliza Dolittle...)

January 16th

Home Sweet Home! Tra-la!Mother was very detached about my Scotland episode – merely said "So glad you had a happy time!" Started hitching home but decided to visit the aunts at Bristol, who stuffed me with egg and fruity cake. Aunt D talks far too much – about herself and her own interests. Under persuasion bought a ticket and went by train.

January 17th

Relaxed in a very hot too - hell - with - utility - bath. Took Mother to a film and later had a spot of beer with Mr G. Eyed with interest an old boy with bright blue eyes and a green hat who sailed around the world in a windjammer in his youth.

January 18th

Loaded with food and accompanied by God's-gift-to-Humanity, boarded the old Slow-and-Doubtful. Felt slightly delirious and talked the most utter rot to two fellow passengers. Criticised the Railways - and then the brutes told me they were railway detectives. However, to show me there was no ill feeling they bought me some tea at Bath.

January 19th

Feel terribly seedy - or groggy - simply bloody, in fact. Why didn't I feel like this yesterday? I would've enjoyed being ill at home.

January 20th

To bed very early. Party being thrown in the cookhouse. Just sufficiently alive to feel disgruntled at missing all the eats - but I wasn't quite forgotten. A few thoughtful women brought some trifle which cooled my burning throat - and sausage rolls and cakes which I didn't dare look at.

January 26th

Poor Peggy looking completely shaken – her fiancée's been killed in the Middle East. I went to Cheltenham to explain matters to Jerry (her American). He is a nice specimen with an attractive grin – good conversationalist too. Pity I'm still half deaf from the recent brief illness: I feel that I missed quite a lot of quips.

January 27th

Felt very high spirited all day. Met Jerry and together we saw Noel Coward's "In which we serve". Peter Fleming's wife has an important part in it. She is a charming woman – appears to be quite conventional but without being stuffy about it.

January 28th

Still struggling with James Agate's "Ego 5". On the whole it's over my head but there are parts that I can appreciate and much of it appeals to my sense of humour. In my extreme youth I used to read this odd little man's Saturday morning articles in the Express. I wonder if I should be so alert, so knowledgeable – and so critical – at 60 something?

January 29th

Agate has hurt me. He's very rude about Oxford (where I was half introduced to him 2 years ago). I'd like to point out to him that one has to be very young – with an unspoiled sense of fun – to enjoy Oxford.

January 30th

Hitched to Worcester, where I met an old Bridgnorthian with whom I had tea. Eventually arrived at B- in state, complete with railway ticket. Richard still at his miserable factory: aunt Cecil still pottering around; piercing glances in my direction; odd woman! Rupert confides that the money that's being spent on the reception (Cecilia's wedding) would buy the chassis of a good lorry. Much chess but no triumphs.

January 31st

Dull day: Richard went to his filthy little job in his beastly little factory and I felt so forsaken. Climbed into my slacks, borrowed a mac and with Bobs, went to meet him at lunchtime. What a weekend! No kisses, no nothing. Feel frustrated. Good lift back which uplifted my dampened spirits. Letter and airgraph from Johnnie (India).

1943			FEBRUARY			1943
M	T	W	T	F	S	S
1	2	3	4	5	6	7
8	9	10	11	12	13	14
15	16	17	18	19	20	21
22	23	24	25	26	27	28

February 1st

Mail from Peggy Lewis (old Bridgnorthian) and May's mother – who sends the odds and ends that I left behind, and also a cake and – ah! Tin of Heinz baked beans – my favourite fruit.

February 2nd

Letter from my mother who sends a letter from the Cunard White Star people – simply grand – Fishface was discharged from hospital as being fit for duty on 21st! Letter from one of Malta's heroic defenders who says "The Shropshire Lad must be a good judge of horse-flesh if he wants to marry you." Went to a fashion-drawing class tonight, which I thoroughly enjoyed.

February 3rd

Parcel from Mrs. G. – and so wonderful – photos from Michael. Studying them brings him so close – and clarifies the memory of him to such an extent, that I know – seriously and eternally it will always be Michael. In the close-ups he appears to have a very deep tan – and his hair looks quite white. In all of them he seems very happy – long of limb and as untidy as ever. Tonight I went out with Peggy and the two Americans. It wasn't particularly good fun.

February 4th

Still spending every free moment with Ella K. Maillart's "Forbidden Journey". She was Peter Fleming's companion on his long trek through China and down to India. She's had – and still is having – a really wonderful and full life. To my delighted surprise, Peter Fleming bears a striking resemblance to Richard. Must remember to remove that particular photo before I return the book to the library.

February 5th

Only one reason to write today. A wired letter arrived from a sailor – unknown to me, but apparently a great friend of my young brother. This man is apparently a stoker on HMS "Turtle": described himself as "five foot nothing and wanted by the police for arson, murder and all sorts of crimes as yet unwritten in the annals of the law." Can't resist sailors. I shall reply – but will also, with much pleasure, beat off my young bro's ears when next we meet.

February 6th

Letter from Richard – very penitent. I feel in urgent need of stimulation: in view of Richard's long hours at the damned factory, I shall have to look elsewhere for it. Last weekend was most disappointing.

February 9th

Joyfully hitched to Oxford where I tea-d at the "Kettle" and chased around for a wedding present. Felt less jubilant when the shop people demanded 18/6d for an inexpensive-looking wooden cruet-affair. Called at Magdalen for my usual "hullo and goodbye" to Scatty and Walter Wagtail and set off again, complete with wedding present in a very dilapidated OHMS envelope. Reached Sloane Sq. at 8.45 pm: hared along to the K.G.T.Q.E Club, dumped my things, painted a new mouth, and tore along the street to the Royal Court. All the B's out: saw only Aunt Cecil gossiping with an old gent in a dog-collar: skedaddled before she spotted me. At closing time, the B. brothers rolled in, escaped at 11.0 pm and slowly walked along Sloane St. – yes! "it was a beauteous, evening calm and free..."

February 10th

My room-mates were 4 Canadian WAAFs – just arrived from the Dominion. Most attractive uniforms – and very attractive girls too. Taxied to the Church, with Father Cronin (the Bridgenorth priest), Richard and the inevitable aunt Cecil. The Quatford people sitting up very primly in their pew (I could feel their eyes boring into my back). Fearfully long ceremony after which Richard and I with a little German trying to keep pace with us, returned to the Royal Court. Richard disappeared frequently – gossiping with odd relations; one particularly objectionable glamour Girl who's supposed to be his cousin. Fiercely whispered to the little German that I was going to scratch her eyes out: he really believed me and frantically tried to reason with me. Got on a tube going the wrong way but staggered thro' Uxbridge at 16.30 hrs and after being shaken into sobriety by the noisiest lorry ever, reached Cheltenham at 20.00 hours.

February 13th

Another odd letter from the stoker-man. Apparently he's 30 and has been in the Navy years an' years. Hopes to earn his living with his voice after the war. Crooner, I suppose. Leonard fell of the ship a few days ago but a sailor fished him out, dried him and sent him home in a boiler suit.

February 14th

Letter from Peggy Syred. She's cursing fiercely about her new station – healthy sign: if she were utterly miserable she wouldn't have sufficient enthusiasm to curse.

February 16th

Most amazing letter from MN. Bro! - this time it's New Zealand. Three continents in four months! I loathe this place even more. He pays tribute to my wanderlust – or adventurous instinct on whatever it is, and says that cousin Doris (who's 6 months younger than I, and has a husband and a baby that looks like a goldfish) is the stupidest woman he knows and "Thank Heavens, your horizon extends beyond a suburban house, a husband and hordes of brats." Poor G. has just had tropical fever – which, he says, is very monotonous.

February 17th

May Henderson writes a long letter reproaching me for my six weeks' silence. This over-sexed young woman is, so she tells me, covered with bruises – the result of a hectic evening with an emotional Yank. Envelope defaced with odd things about "Grenadier Guards" and "Thanks for the memory" – in commemoration of our last leave.

February 19th

Sixth boy-friend about to beetle off to Canada. David's in the RAF – hops around from it WO to Navigation Schools, and RAF. Regiment schools. I wonder what he is going to be? Airmail from MN. Bro': poor dear is stuck in Egypt – near the Suez Canal – without a ship. However – there is a Greek girl – a refugee – to cheer his lonely hours.

February 22nd

Letter from the mighty S/Lt Vince who threatens to seduce me at our next meeting. Hah! Drank beer with Jerry Charm (Peggy's American friend) in Cheltenham tonight. Amusing person.

February 23rd

Tramped along, feeling very empty, hoping for a lift. Hopes rewarded. The driver of a very snooty looking car accused me of being the most extraordinary woman he'd ever met. Aunt D. as vociferous as ever. Can tolerate her while she provides such good food. On return journey a young man on a bicycle introduced himself: no lifts so adjourned to the nearest pub. Later picked up by a fireman (without an engine). At 10.30 pm, still 20 miles from camp. Philosophically picknicked middle of road until the inevitable lorry roared up – as I knew it would.

February 24th

A sweet letter from Michael who wants the merest glimpse of me before I go gallivanting around the world. I've airmailed back that even the merest glimpse would be fatal to my wonderful plans. Pays me one of his very rare compliments "a lovable, persistently attractive WAAF". But the most wonderful news of all is that he may be allowed to fly after all.

February 25th

Mild sort of binge – Maggie Botwright off to a bomber station tomorrow. Spent an hour at "The Chosen" drinking rough cider and beer and later called in at "Smoky Joe's" for a meal. Maggie in such a condition that she collapsed and spent a penny outside Station Headquarters. Oh! For the Group Captain to be in his office!

February 26th

A very amusing letter from Beryl Holt-Bush brightened what would've been a very dull day. The screwy specimen is now in Dundee, Scotland: amusing herself with a three-ringed bloke, whiskey is plentiful, too – ah! I feel a thirst coming on! Drank lager with "Nose" (alias Jackson) whose conversation is limited to "How many men have you driven mad, Beautiful?" Grandma (wing off.) is taking an interest in me – to my utter horror says she can't fathom me – feel rather pleased to think that I baffle a woman whose word is law to several thousand WAAF. Relieved when little chat was disturbed by telephone ringing.

February 27th

My once beloved and "ever-faithful" Richard has deserted me. Can't decide whether to rejoice or be sad. Neither of us has written since the brief collision at the wedding. I haven't any time to think sad and sentimental thoughts – there's so much to do.

February 28th

Took my lonely self to the camp cinema this afternoon: saw the exquisitely funny "Turtles of Tahiti." Life portrayed is my ideal existence: wonder if I shall ever have the opportunity? Tea in Cheltenham and then to the Town Hall to hear the Spa Orchestra – which was most disappointing. Jerry describes it as "corny". Feel the Americans have words for everything. English vocabulary too limited – too stilted.

1943			MARCH			1943
M	T	W	T	F	S	S
1	2	3	4	5	6	7
8	9	10	11	12	13	14
15	16	17	18	19	20	21
22	23	24	25	26	27	28
29	30	31	..	..	..	..

March 1st

Letter from Peggy – as hilarious and as full of fun as ever – even Gt. Yarmouth hasn't quietened her – thank Heavens. She encloses a photo of a Yank whom she is trying to sell me – or perhaps I'm the one who's being sold. Peggy's business transactions are so complicated.

March 2nd

Changed Gillian's Xmas book token for Lella Secor Florence's "My Goodness!, my Passport." I think I shall like it. Didn't enjoy the art evening tonight – wrong mood: too tired. With Marjorie to the cinema to see "The Male Animal." Vaguely amusing. An intense young American quoted a line or two from Rupert Brooke's "When love has changed to kindliness..." – but without understanding. I suppose one has to be middle-aged and ten-years-married to understand.

March 3rd

Contemplating taking some sort of drastic measures to get out of this place. Two courses are open – a posting: trying for the new job – Cypher. Have decided to try both; in view of the watch keeping flop of a year ago, I don't hold out much hope for the remustering. However, I feel too desperate to allow any opportunity, however slight, to pass by without doing something.

March 4th

Wonderful letter from Michael: the endearing phrases have been floating through my head all day. "There'll never be another Mrs. M-B. but you..." with Jerry to hear Pouishnoff. A truly satisfying recital, which I enjoyed as much as any full orchestral concert. When he played my beloved military Polonaise, I wanted to stand up and cheer as the excitement surged through me. Adjourned to Kate's afterwards, where Jerry gave me a long and amusing account of his studio days in Greenwich Village.

March 5th

Jackson confined to camp for some obscure crime; however, he managed to get out on someone else's pass. So far, I've managed to tolerate his attitude of undiluted adoration, but it's beginning to irritate me intensely. I know I'm a miserable, unreasonable cuss but there must be some other woman in Cheltenham who'd like him more that I.

March 6th

News from Johnnie at last. He doesn't really seem very happy about India even now. He's still enthusing about his return to England and the fun we'll have. Apparently he's chosen to deliberately ignore my pointed remarks in previous letters: must airgraph him yet again that I won't be in England. Mother already making plans for visits to relations on my next leave. Spent two brief hours with Jerry Charm tonight.

March 7th

Unwillingly to Cheltenham to drink lager (with a spot of whiskey) with Jackson. Am desperately seeking a way out as I've no desire to see him again. Very difficult indeed.

March 8th

Passionate letter from Freddie; the stoker, also interesting little note from Johnnie's sister, Sheila. Spent the evening at a Gramopera Club in Cheltenham, whence one of the women dragged me. Evening's programme was 2nd act of "The Valkyrie" – Familiar strains of "The Ride" filled me with nostalgia for Oxford – Magdalen – Donald's rooms – the deer park – the window seat – the eternal trees – and sunshine streaming through the branches.

March 9th

Such wonderful news – Aubrey back from Malta. Home this weekend – the hussy returns to Dorset – la! La! Feel that it's not true, somehow – but it is – a letter from him, postmarked "Poole."

March 10th

No letters in but managed to finish an 18-page screed to Joan – long overdue. Feel hectically excited about the weekend. Cynical trait warns that it may be a flop. Scribbled notes to the two Americans cancelling dates. Saw the recommendation for my remustering to "Cypher". Refuse to allow my optimistic spirit to soar too high. However – it may be a means of escape.

March 11th

'nother letter from Michael: also one airmail and two cards from Johnnie. Mother's letter containing ten precious shillings has been censored – ha! Bullied into sewing red curtains as a delightful little pastime for domestic night!

March 12th

Feel quite convinced that all the local clocks have been slowed up – hurry up, tomorrow, for I must away – over the hills to Dorset to greet my own heroic defender of Malta...

March 13th

4½ hrs. continuous hitching and then late tea at a pub at Evercreech and the night train to Dorset. Aubrey very brown: only visible alteration, numerous white hairs. His sense of fun remains unchanged. Eventually reached bed at 0500 hrs – whew! Such a session: but it made good hearing.

March 14th

The two letters from Michael were wonderful. He says "I love your phraseology and your apt and sometime somewhat cynical little sentences. Then your poignantly sweet sentimentalism comes out, to my great delight..." He promises not to run away if I am "in a marriageable state" when he returns. But there won't be time for such things. At 9.30 am leaped out of bed, into slacks, sweater, and then, lazily ambled down to Sandbanks – with Aubrey, of course. Sunbathed with my slacks-legs rolled up to my knees, Swigged the merest spot of gin at Capt. Harrington's Bungalow and allowed myself to be made passionate love to. A. says that "it was worth waiting 22 months..." Arrived home at 19.30 hours...

March 15th

Usual tearing around the house, collecting odds and ends to take back. Usual difficulty in persuading Leonard (who now bears the honourable title of "prefect") to go to school. As the train started, Aubrey gallantly and recklessly leapt upon the running board for one last friendly salute. Sunshine too tempting so I hopped out at Evercreech and hitched to Bristol, where I fell foul of a female ticket collector who thought I'd travelled without a ticket. Train seems even more tame after the glorious uncertainty of hitching.

March 16th

Chocolate and liquorice allsorts from the generous stoker - Freddie Gossling who begs me to go home next weekend. Have replied, expressing eternal regret at having missed him last weekend.

March 17th

Sent a very glamorous birthday card to the old man – who may not think it at all funny although I dislike him intensely I send him a card from sheer habit. I feel that to ignore his birthday would be rather brutal – although there'll come a time when we shall be more than brutal to him.

March 19th

Sweet letter from Aubrey who considers that he "ruddy well knows more about the qualities of our Griffin than the stupid WAAF "

March 20th

Usual routine day: alas! No mail. No excitement whatsoever. Queued for a bus for Cheltenham; gave up the ghost after ½ hour – even the lure of Dennis Puleston at the Canary Islands couldn't hypnotise me into braving the mist and the chill air so I betook myself to the hut where I scorched my beautiful pins in front of a roaring fire.

March 22nd

Another rare red-letter today. The mail brought an airmail from Johnnie (who hasn't seen a white woman for four months): an out-of-date letter from Malta – with a choice final sentence – "here's to scantier scanties" – and – two airgraphs from Michael who says that my letters "are a great source of happiness" to him.

March 23rd

Kathleen is a "potential NCO". My God! No more shall I take her down to Dorset. I have to tolerate quite sufficient ribbing now. She says that I was extremely ungrateful about the Xmas present – Yes! The awful Godfrey Winn book. I still can't understand why Kay, of all people, should thrust such a thing upon me. I shudder when I see it with my poetry and travel books – one blessing, I can't see the title as I've stuck it up back to front. I think I may be a literary snob – or do I? or am I?

March 24th

A letter from Jerry (the American) at teatime, urging me to meet him tonight. Hastily persuaded someone to do my duty and dashed out for a bus. Pleasant evening: I like an occasional date with him but regular meetings annoy me.

March 26th

So Scranny Baker is still alive. Letter dated December arrived too. He is as sweet and as flattering as ever. Oh! that Michael were as complimentary – or as observant?? – but then – he wouldn't be Michael, I suppose. His very blindness endears him to me.

March 27th

Blue, blue sky, white woolly clouds – and such sunshine. Cycled to RAF. Staverton[1] where I played a speedy game of netball - and helped to win.

---

[1] RAF Staverton was about 4 miles north of Cheltenham.

March 28th

Wasted an hour of a perfect day hammering a typewriter and scanning the headlines. After lunch, changed into sports kit, and with the RAF hockey team, rode in state to RAF Station, to lick the netball team by 22-5 goals, and eat an enormous tea.

March 29th

The wind howls, the rain lashes, there is no fire in the hut and Nancy, Barbara and I are completely and utterly cheesed. Our efforts to bag three 6d. seats at the 'flicks' are fruitless so – we wearily trudge through the puddles to "Smoky Joe's" where we spend our last shillings on sausages and chips.

March 30th

My efforts have been rewarded – Vince knows something about Yachts! He says that he's owned them from 15 to 120 tons! I had an idea that he was the right man for this cruising scheme... Aubrey is back at Worthy Down – where he was stationed nearly 3 years ago – ah! Andover!

March 31st

Airgraph from David (Canada) Awful scrawl – even worse on microscopic airgraphs. Is much amused by Canada : threatens to send a photo of himself in "Yukon" attire.

1943			APRIL			1943
M	T	W	T	F	S	S
..	..	..	1	2	3	4
5	6	7	8	9	10	11
12	13	14	15	16	17	18
19	20	21	22	23	24	25
26	27	28	29	30	..	..

April 1st

Today achieved what my sceptical friends believe to be impossible – heroically put a pound in my savings book. To-date it bears a pathetic entry – "Deposit 15/-" "Demand 13/-" Ah! 22/- towards a yacht – or at least a haversack for the Great Hitching venture.

April 2nd

Hag no. 2 – otherwise Scatty Gover of Devonshire – has suddenly become engaged to a sailor whom she knows only vaguely – but nothing is definite as far as that odd – but delightful woman is concerned… I'd always imagined that she was hopelessly and irredeemably doomed to alcoholically-happy spinsterhood. Ha! How I misjudge people – and how blind I am to their possibilities! Played hockey tonight: being completely ignorant of the rules I hesitated to be too dashing: managed to hit the ball several times.

April 3rd

Nothing happens: I work extraordinarily hard and am rewarded by a letter from mother who feels sentimental because Leonard is 14 today. Phoned Greetings telegrams to him and to Gillian's offspring Jennifer who attains the noble age of 11 tomorrow.

April 4th

Effie demands her tennis racquet – damn! That means a visit to Bridgnorth. Her letter cheered me a little but this afternoon, I feel utterly desolate. The sun shines – and I have to hammer a typewriter for 7 long, dreary hours.

April 5th

News from Peggie Syred now in Newcastle. She's feeling rather "cheesed", I gather. I think – I'm sure – I'd hate Newcastle. Cities – smoke – grime – smug people. Oh for the sea – sunlight dancing on the waves – clean air.

April 6th

Hah! Richard writes – or rather scrawls in pencil. Sweet thing – quite vague but ends "always". Matthewman (nice woman) tried to rope me in for a Brains Trust session but I managed to squiggle out of it. Heavens! I should've expired from fright – to face such an audience of intellectual-looking young women. I enjoyed it, as one of the spectators, but as a "trustee" – whew! I shudder to think of it.

April 7th

I feel so pleased – the pound is still safe in the Post Office. I've proved that I can do it – I shall repeat the performance again and again, until I have sufficient to help me to realise my heart's desire.

April 8th

The wings off. has accused me of not aiming for something. Says I'm intelligent and can't understand why I don't take a pride in my appearance. My tongue clove to the roof of my mouth: I didn't dare utter a word because I was so utterly miserable and I knew that, under her well meant sympathy, I should weep or do something equally awful. I must get off this depot.

April 9th

Reams of nonsense from his mirthful majesty, Scranny Baker. Includes a beautiful poem dedicated to me. Must send a copy to Michael – just to keep him up to scratch.

April 10th

Rather dull letter from Eileen Williams (sergeant in Sussex): she's losing the knack of humorous letter-writing.

April 11th

Worked very hard all day – which means another 24 hrs. escape sometime in the distant future. Stooged around the hut this evening. Achieved nothing – which wasn't surprising.

April 12th

Gillian has written that there's a vacancy at Torquay – would I like to go? Spot of quick thinking and some swift juggling with the file containing applications for a posting – and, hey presto! Mine won't be dealt with for at least another week. Will give the Devonshire one time to come thru', Hugh (late "Ajax" commander: Nick's present husband) is at Plymouth. I have visions of fun and games with the Navy-braid and brandy. Brighter prospect than being isolated in the Dorset wilds.

April 13th

Mother sends two letters from Fishface. Such old letters – "December – Australia". No further news so presume that he's still stuck at Suez. Mrs. G. (bless her!) accusing me of not writing to Vince sufficiently frequently. Ha! He's beautiful – and a sub-loot – what more can he desire? Bet he has hordes of women in every port. Apparently Leonard has casually mentioned to her that he had ½ pt bitter in a local pub. Mother blithely says "He's joking." Bet he's not.

April 14th

6d worth of mirth at the camp cinema tonight. That shocking specimen Mickey Rooney in a "Yank at Eton". I love his facial contortions. The Eton scenes were vaguely reminiscent of Oxford – but not so sufficiently so to make me nostalgic.

April 15th

Ambled along to the NAAFI to view the dance being held there. Saw a girl who very strongly reminded me of someone at school. She was then small and plump with a fringe. Eventually asked her if she knew Dorset – half – cynically expected her to disclaim, with a Lancashire accent, that she'd never heard of it. But she had – and she was the girl. Felt very pleased. Became involved with a rather stewed American. To save money Babs & I drank deserted drinks in the Games Rm. I become slightly stewed and concluded the revelry by sitting on the hut steps with Alabama, eating very greasy chips.

April 16th

Oh! Such a fat letter from home – no: not a letter - an envelope with magic contents – three letters from Johnnie (India): an airgraph from Scranny (South Africa) and – final and greatest blessing a January letter from Michael. "You're a strange creature dearest, very odd mixture." And then – "I think I like you best – the real you – not the semi-sophisticated actress, Dorothy Griffin – just you." Michael awakes – and his magic words fill me with supreme happiness. Drank a little with the cheery Jerry Charm tonight. Ambled around Pittville Park in Cheltenham. Jerry completely enchanted by England in Spring and the wonderful colours of the pheasants in the park.

April 17th

The Adjutant bodes farewell – thank goodness. She made a tour of the orderly room, saying the usual banal things – to me – "Hope you have your props soon." Blah! (rude noise!)

April 18th

Letter containing a slightly obscene poem from that old closet in officer's uniform, Beryl Holt-Brush. She encloses a letter from the estate agents – who're trying to sting us 12 guineas a week for a house in Sandbanks. I suppose she gave them the impression that we want a damned great mansion. After lunch, relaxed in the sun! By sundown had acquired the foundation of a gorgeous South American complexion. My skin feels tight when I laugh. Thanked the dear sun for such a good days' work. With Nancy and the incorrigible Babs ambled along to Smokey Joe's for chips and peas and orange juice. A very satisfying day.

April 19th

Long, long epistle from Aubrey who begins "Dearest Squiff" – and accuses me of being "an absolute darling". I do like him and I'm glad that he's survived eight years of knowing me. Note from Gillian, she's done the necessary from her end regarding my posting to Torquay. Pip-pip for Devonshire! Oh, the sheer heaven of it – to get away from this woman-infested existence, to make a fresh start, with Gillian to push me into things. I think I'll wash a uniform – it may not improve much but I shall feel smugly righteous.

April 20th

It's high time that I heard from that philandering sailor, S/Lt George Vince, RNVR. Dammit! It's nine days since I wrote. I suppose he's busy with his old barge, or something equally footling. With Nancy to the inevitable escape – the camp cinema. Found the film particularly interesting. The heroine (?) was refreshingly vixenish – a type that appeals to me. Sick of simpering females.

April 21st

Very funny letter from Peggy Syred. Did my old heart good to read it. Almost rejuvenated me. She's debating whether to marry some filthily rich bloke – he's a dear little airman. God! I hope he's an improvement on the specimens in this dump. And yet – they wouldn't arouse any interest in my resentful heart if they were Adonises and Apollos. I think I am growing old or growing up or something equally depressing.

April 22nd

Letters from Marion and May, the two old Scots besoms. Marion has accepted Hugh's proposal. I don't object – at the moment, as he's safely stuck in the Middle East. But if he should return before we're away on our travels? - I won't even think of it! Another airmail from India: Johnnie is incorrigible. He's now resolving to write twice a week. This is the end! I can barely keep pace with him now. Managed to produce two airmail lettercards to him tonight: I know he's the most deserving of the pathetic cases overseas.

April 23rd

And yet another letter from Aubrey (ex-Malta). Seems something has bitten him – most complicated if it's the inevitable love-bug. He's a dear thing: describes a cycle ride to Wimborne, a nap in a hedge and a feast of raw Swedes, poached from a field. Tonight, occupied my usual front pew at the camp cinema. Found the film very funny. Thrilling newsreel of the American and British armies in North Africa. The irony of it – I joined up to find adventure - and I'm still seeking it. There's a possibility of our going overseas: I have determined to avoid it. After waiting 22 years, I can surely hang on for another year or two, to see the world outside of England.

April 24th

A postal order from Dad and a brief and not very cheering letter from my mother. During the writing of a letter to Michael, lost control somewhat and told him a little of my real feelings regarding his flying. I know it's an unwise thing to do but Michael may find it enlightening – probably amusing, too.

April 25th

Strap me! Stuck in quarantine because some woman's contracted diphtheria. Managed to hear this afternoon's symphony concert however.

April 26th

This quarantine biz. is a good thing – breakfast brought to the hut – first time I've eaten porridge in bed in camp. Someone attacked by the organising urge so we found ourselves route-marching. Didn't mind as the countryside is particularly beautiful at this time of year.

April 27th

Beginning to take a dim view of this quarantine: we have to work! We have a special room assigned to us: in a burst of wit I printed a label "Beware! Leper colony" and affixed it to the door. My artist's sense has been wounded: the label has been removed. Acted as guinea-pigs for the medical people who've injected some stuff into our arms. Everyone pseudo-heroic.

April 28th

And yet another letter from my beloved "Dusty" - now a P.O. in the Fleet Air Arm and still in Winchester. In a sudden burst of magnanimity, he addresses me as "Sweet one - darling beloved." Would be quite flattered - if I didn't realise that he probably had his tongue in his cheek when he wrote these words. Promises to come to Dorset - if only for a flying visit on my next leave. Signs himself "Yours in blossomtime..."

April 29th

Whoopee! Two photos of the incredibly beautiful Michael - ye Gods, I daren't look at him - I reiterate "a disturbing influence". On one he has quoted my famous words - "Yes - perhaps in 5.000 years - who knows?" Sometimes I wish I could just glimpse into the future: and yet even that would deprive life of its joy - the unexpectedness - happiness - and the brief pain. When I am 70 or so (and I have no doubt that I shall be allowed to live until this great age) it'll be wonderfully interesting to meditate on the years that have passed and the minor triumphs that can never be re-lived - except in one's thoughts.

April 30th

A few words from Gillian - written on huge notepaper. I feel rather moved by her apparent eagerness to see me in Torquay. Says that she hopes I shall be down in time to join their next "wings for Victory" parade. I damned well hope I won't. And if I am, I'll try my very best to get out of it. Says Hugh has found a 'hen-house' to live in. It's really a chalet in the grounds of a Guest House. Luxury-loving Gillian refuses to have anything to do with it. I shall offer my services to him - he's so sweet and patient: just the person to tolerate my efforts.

1943			MAY			1943
M	T	W	T	F	S	S
..	..	..	..	..	1	2
3	4	5	6	7	8	9
10	11	12	13	14	15	16
17	18	19	20	21	22	23
24/31	25	26	27	28	29	30

May 1st

No mail – but I contrived to make this day a day to remember. Arranged to have the afternoon off, and while everyone else was out route-marching, I stretched out on someone's bed and heard a broadcast of Beethoven's Fourth. The dim ones returned half-way through the symphony and one particularly objectionable specimen actually dared to approach the radio with the intention of changing the station. I defended the radio and delivered a short speech: I felt their glares – but stood my ground and heard the last two movements with fierce pride and exultation.

May 2nd

Last night's party in the hut must be the explanation for the extraordinary, happy and contented feeling that pervades my restless being this morning. I think that the fact that we made it a good party against such overwhelming odds – no alcohol, complete absence of one mere male, and after a week's c.c.[1] – is sure proof that there's some spirit left in this "happy breed".

May 5th

First day of freedom – and what happens? – stooge No. 1 works. The other inmates of the hut merrily stagger in at 10.30 pm happily slewed and I am absolutely sober and quite miserable.

May 6th

To the "Hare and Hounds" with a few bright specimens who plan to reduce me to a state of alcoholic helplessness. The effervescent Louie introduces her famous game "Toss penny" and soon we find ourselves frantically competing against two melancholy Australians, with several Canadian P/O navigators as spectators at 10.15 pm. I find myself wandering down the lane, with a pocketful of pennies and a P/O as escort. Very young, very blond – but I was atrociously rude to him which was a shame as he even liked poetry!

[1] C.C. - Confined to camp.

May 7th

Half-day to cycle to Cheltenham where I spent far too much money. Book of cartoons and some startlingly blue stationery for Kay; a book of poems for Peggy; birthday telegrams to three people. Cycling with the irrepressible Jerry Charm tonight, vicious thunderstorm which soaked us and annoyed Mr. C and amused me. Dragged him into Smoky Joe's for sausages and chips, which, I have a feeling, was the last straw.

May 8th

To the "H. and H." but there was no sign of the blonde Canadian P/O. Perhaps I was rather glad as it might have been embarrassing to face him after my behaviour.

May 9th

Cycling with the amusing Jerry Charm. Wore down my resistance by his continual pleadings to see me with my hair down, so – I let it flow: result – "Gee, Squiff! You look like a woman!" On the return journey, Mother Nature put on a terrific show which slightly dampened the sunny Mr. C.'s enthusiasm – thunder and such rain. I soon became soaked – and enjoyed it. Not so the U.S. Army. Even sausages and chips (for which I footed the bill) at Smoky Joe's restored his good spirits. So what?

May 10th

Letter from Strawberry Tart – now in Northern Ireland. I take a dim view of this. One of my lovers returns from overseas and after a few weeks, he is whisked off again. He takes a dim view, too. For the sake of my rapidly- failing virginity, I hope they don't keep him away 22 months.

May 14th

Letter from bro' George – still shore-bound at Suez. He's not starving, homeless and broke as mother indulgently fears he is. The Greek girl is very pretty but doesn't take him "seriously". Signs himself the "black sheep." (I wonder what's stirred his conscience!)

May 15th

As a result of my afternoon's relaxing in bright sunshine, have acquired an impressive South American complexion. In the cool of the evening, cycled to Cheltenham with Nancy. Found a fair: temptation too great so gracefully succumbed and rode around on a few things. Unlucky with darts. Bought chips at an evil-smelling shop. At the 'Y' was spotted by a bright young American from Alabama whom I met at a camp dance. Result – date tomorrow night.

May 16th

Am I frustrated! Apparently "Alabama" is not of the stuff that horses are made – he lacks patience. I arrive an hour later and he is not there... However!

May 17th

Good show of cards and telegrams. Celebrated my 22nd anniversary (such a noble age!) by feeling extremely ill this morning and brimful of high spirits this afternoon. With several women, saw the exotic Carmen Miranda in her latest technicolour effort. At midnight, gorged ham sandwiches in Heathie's bunk.

May 18th

Registered mail from my never-forgetful mother – money and overseas mail. A fat airmail letter from Michael – includes a beautiful poem by a pilot, recently killed. It is gay, light-hearted, with a touch of the immortal – of such stuff are bird-men made.

May 19th

Michael's letter of yesterday was obviously written when he was in a particularly anti-everything mood, with his biting tongue, he lashes at the Americans, British politics – and, of course, at me, too.

May 22nd

Lorry-jumped to Bridgnorth where I was warmly welcomed – even the stolid Richard arousing from his usual state of semi-lethargy. He and Rupert made a good job of upsetting beer over my blue frock: I was not impressed by their effusive apologies.

May 23rd

Attired in some rather attractive borrowed rags – royal blue sweater and socks and grey skirt – rowed up the river with the B. bros. Rode back to Glos. in an American truck – driven by a magnificent specimen of American negro.

May 24th

Such news! – I go to Torquay on Thursday. Have I any regrets? No sirree!!! I've become quite accustomed to loving people – and leaving 'em. Must feverishly pack – why "feverishly"? - in keeping with the old tradition, you know.

May 26th

To commemorate my second last evening in this particularly "blessed spot" I attended a rookies' concert in the NAAFI. It was amazingly good – largely due to the originality of three girls recently arrived from South America, and also the efforts of a typical little Dutch girl with the most fascinating accent.

May 27th

Away to Cheltenham to see the enchanting Jerry Charm, of course, I am 1 ¾ hrs. late and, of course, he isn't there. I returned to Innsworth – but not feeling depressed. Living in anticipation, I can't feel anything but very happy. Wired Gillian regarding my possible arrival at 14.00 hours. Nancy A. seems rather miserable: she's not yet acclimatised to this loving' and leavin' business, I fear.

May 28th

After a hundred farewells to half-awake people, I was off – to begin a new episode in my Service life. Spent several hours at Bristol gorging chocolate cake and poached eggs at the aunt's house. Loaded with food and flowers and much luggage, left for Torquay. Arrived several hours late to hear that friend Gillian was away on sick leave but returns next week. Shamelessly hared off to a dance – barely three hours after my belated arrival. So many men that I wanted to pinch them to make sure that they weren't merely mirages. Was brought back to the hostel by a very youthful cadet who is leaving on Saturday. First time – I draw a blank.

1943			JUNE			1943
M	T	W	T	F	S	S
..	1	2	3	4	5	6
7	8	9	10	11	12	13
14	15	16	17	18	19	20
21	22	23	24	25	26	27
28	29	30	..	..	..	..

June 1st

I patiently wait for mail – but there is none – yet. However, Sheila and I tootled off to a dance at the "Grand". There I met a rather small – and terribly young cadet who remembers me as a wild young woman in a filthy mac, skimming around the town on a bone shaker, lugging a sack of straw. He persuaded me to jigger around the floor with him until a long and lean cadet murmured that John was waiting outside. Decided not to go but – went. J tried to entice me out to a meal but I heroically refused and succeeded in luring him in to dance. I fox-trotted, quick-stepped and waltzed quite satisfyingly. If John had held me any closer people would've accused us of committing misconduct in public, I feel sure.

June 2nd

Ah! My very exotic swim-suit has arrived and such a wad of mail! India, the Middle East, North Africa, Canada – and a book-token from Gillian; also an amusing book from Donald (ex-Oxford) who tersely wishes me a happy birthday. Odd person – I haven't heard from him for months – and yet he remembers my birthday. I am bloody browned off at the moment! I've worked up into a receptive mood for Beethoven's 9th – and now I've been ejected from the room because some damned unimportant lecture is being held there. My God! I shall never recover!

June 5th

On duty – Long talk with flight – who spun long stories of his escapades as an AC2.

June 6th

With Sheila and the bright young cadets, tramped into the country to a pseudo-antique pub called the "Drum" where we quaffed much cider which did verily much affect us. Later danced at the weird "Cockington Club". Marked the occasion by bunging John's cap into a water-tank.

June 7th

A dull day so – no swimming – for the timid RAF and WAAF. To the cinema this evening with Sheila and two of the young men. John is feeling smugly righteous about the extreme virtue of our beautiful friendship. Ha! Little does he guess!

June 8th

Michael writes: "I haven't quite got there to put in my claim for you!" and "I love you very much, my darling." Could I ask for anything more?

June 10th

With Gillian to see "Star Spangled Rhythm". Amusing – but only in places. Coffee at the Palm Court afterwards. G. assures me that she flew to Washington and back during her stay at Prestwick. Difficult to believe – but it's feasible as she's such an incredible woman.

June 12th

Cider session at the "Railway Inn" – awful den. All extremely merry.

June 13th

Jack Stewart's farewell binge. Only amusing thing was a most odd sergeant who poured motherly advice into my unsympathetic ear. He was convinced that I was on the verge of seduction by the unattractive Jack.

June 14th

On duty at the Abbey – where I slept, but not even a glimpse of the notorious ghost.

June 15th

Danced at the "Grand". The "Archduke" bores me but I shall continue to honour him with my company until such time as I get organised.

June 16th

Home - after losing identity card en route. Polyphotos enlargements arrived - don't like them. Mother very pleased - as usual. Mother and L. most insistent upon my entering for tonight's beauty contest. I did - but didn't get anywhere. First prize winner most attractive but others awful bags. Apparently our entry and exit on the stage counted - and I hurried too much, which wasn't surprising. My confidence in myself remains unshaken.

June 17th

Very dull day. I feel lost - and rather miserable. Why, I wander? Letter from Aubrey H. - back in Northern Ireland again.

June 18th

Bags of mail - one from Jerry Charm (U.S.) who describes me as "the most irresponsible, undependable calloused female" he's ever met. One from Richard (now Fleet Air Arm); one from Beryl H-B.

June 19th

Leonard who persuaded me that he was the Fred Astaire of Dorset, hasn't the faintest knowledge of how to dance. Mother danced for the first time in 24 years. I danced with several people - none of them particularly interesting.

June 20th

To that flea-pit - the "Amity" with mother and dear old uncle Joe.

June 21st

To "Neguri[1]" where I sunbathed and made full use of the Captain's gramophone. Have given mother a message for him "Dear Captain H., I am very disappointed in your choice of records."

June 22nd

Afternoon at "Neguri". Still feeling very lonely: something is lacking. I am so puzzled: I've analysed my feelings but can reach no satisfactory conclusion.

June 23rd

Visited some relations whom I found less dull than the rest. Cousin Vivienne full of beans – quite interesting.

June 24th

To Bournemouth, where I spent 3 coupons and an unnecessary amount of money. Found an amusing book for Michael "Clipped Wings" being a "pictorial diary of incidents in the life of an unrecognised airman."

June 25th

I feel almost relieved to be back. Why didn't I enjoy my leave? Didn't I adjust myself? Or is it loneliness? Or dullness? I don't know. Scooted along to the Pavilion to meet Sheila, Maud and Ken who'd been to see Tauber in "Old Chelsea". Lager at the "Palm Court."

---

[1] Name of house in Sandbanks.

June 26th

After an afternoon of sunshine, we all went haywire on a cider session. Both the Johns very slewed. One rushing around politely enquiring of suburban householders "Where is the nearest field?" – until two people invited him in to use theirs.

June 27th

Dizzy morning. Afternoon in the sun on the roof of the Abbey. Long chat with the Duty officer who panicked when the siren wailed.

June 30th

Was duly charged and tried for WOAS[1] losing by neglect, one dilapidated identity card. Awarded 3 days c.c. Tonight amused myself by cleaning lavatories, baths, and performing other highly-skilled and delicate jobs.

---

[1] WOAS: Whilst on active service

1943			JULY			1943
M	T	W	T	F	S	S
..	..	..	1	2	3	4
5	6	7	8	9	10	11
12	13	14	15	16	17	18
19	20	21	22	23	24	25
26	27	28	29	30	31	..

July 1st

Programme for tonight – sweeping steps outside hostel, tidying up the garden and cleaning windows. But – as I never tired of assuring my appreciative audience, it all constituted an interesting experience!

July 2nd

A five-month old letter from my dashing brother : two photos enclosed. He's oh so thin – but very grown-up. Heard Beethoven's 2nd and Tchaikovsky's "Swan Lake" tonight. The "Archduke" and another cadet paid a surprise visit. The warder gave me some cider, as a result of which I had to creep through the darkened corridors at 04.20 in search of the lavatory.

July 3rd

Quantity of mail from Johnnie, Scranny (two airgraphs about a rich and handsome widow), letter from a woman to whom I wrote 5 months ago. Sun-bathed this afternoon with the usual gang. Visited the "Drum" tonight: cider, shandy, ginger wine – and roses from the railway station.

July 4th

Sunbathing this afternoon. Interesting little group of Poles quite near. With the two Johns, washed dishes in a canteen this evening.

July 5th

Odd sort of an evening – a woman in an incredible hat gave us a pep-talk on religion. Descendant of Salvation Army founder. High spot – as far as I was concerned was a Chopin Etude. Hoped – but in vain – that she might play more.

July 9th

Dancing on the Spa where Chris Davies (That Man from Brazil) bought whiskey for me and my thirsty cronies. Feel vaguely interested in T.M.F.B. Have promised to take him on a cider session sometime. Spent the rest of the evening with a wild Scots cadet from the Far East who performed various endearing little tricks such as lifting me in the air and urging me to bite his ear.

July 10th

With the gang to the "Drum" where I had a mild flirtation with a Polish commissioned type: culminated in my drinking ginger wine with him while the Archduke marched out in high dudgeon. Refused the Pole's offer to take me back as I cynically suspect an ulterior motive. Later effected a reconciliation with the Archduke.

July 11th

To church to pray for the merchant Navy – with special thoughts for my own precious G., who's sailing the high seas. To the flicks with the gang this evening.

July 12th

A most beautiful sight – a pound box of chocolates from David (who's in Canada). I resigned myself to sharing them with numerous orderly room personnel and room-mates.

July 14th

Gillian Nicholson accuses me of having a Peter Pan complex as far as boy-friends are concerned. Deeply hurt to think that she misunderstands my great maternal instinct.

July 16th

Free ticket for dancing at the Spa where to my chagrin, I saw T.M.F.B. providing whiskey for a gang of wretched WAAFs. Again met the Scots cadet from the Far East, and made an effort to forget T.M.F.B. His apparent lack of interest intrigues me.

July 17th

Sheila's massive Scot has arrived. Gang out in full force. All adjourned to the "Railway Inn", where one and all flung darts in all directions and lapped up prodigious quantities of cider. S's m.S. a very attractive person: I like his sense of humour.

July 19th

Heard from May Hen., who has become whole-heartedly involved with a Pole. Lor'! I must get me a Continental!

July 20th

Spent such a dull evening with my Air Sea Rescue type (just back from Iceland). Apparently he's a virgin (I wot not the male equivalent – but he's IT) – a fact, sufficient in itself to repel me. Extraordinarily dull young man, I fear. I shattered his illusions, when I casually mentioned that I made a practice of sleeping with the Boy-friends on leave as I thought they deserved something.

July 22nd

Phone call from Beryl H-B., who has been robbed of £5 by a callous F/LT. Apparently he presented her with a cheque that bounced. B. proposes a rendezvous in Town next month. Idea doesn't particularly appeal – but at least it would be amusing.

July 23rd

Authority has been received for the owner of this diary to decorate her uniform with one Good Conduct Stripe – yea! Three years' undetected crime. Now my pay will increase with the magnificent increment of 2d. per diem.

July 24th

The planned Big Binge given by the gang in honour of Sheila's massive Scot's last night did not materialise, so I hied me to the Abbey, where I was overcome by hysterical giggles (induced by Mrs.Yea) and laughed at the duty officer: whereupon I hastily exited from the room.

July 25th

With Betty (who has two free tickets) to a tennis tournament. Several champs playing: all disappointing. But I enjoyed relaxing in the best seats, while the WAAF officer stood with the less fortunate spectators.

July 26th

Scranny's 15th May effort has arrived. His philosophy and outlook on life make the whole thing seem a great game – and fun. I love Michael – but living with Scranny would be grand.

July 27th

At 20.30 hours, I abandoned my feeble attempt at swotting, flung on my tunic and antiquated chapeau, and with Maud and Selina (a new woman) sauntered through the town to a canteen for grapefruit and tomato sandwiches.

July 28th

Still feverishly trying to cram form numbers and such-like into my reluctant mind. I find it difficult to gauge my success even at this stage.

July 29th

Odd – but this is the first anniversary of my one and only trade test – and tonight, I sat for another as a sort of celebration. The Scots F/Sgt. was very lenient and I have every reason to hope for the best. Ho! Ho! A step up at last.

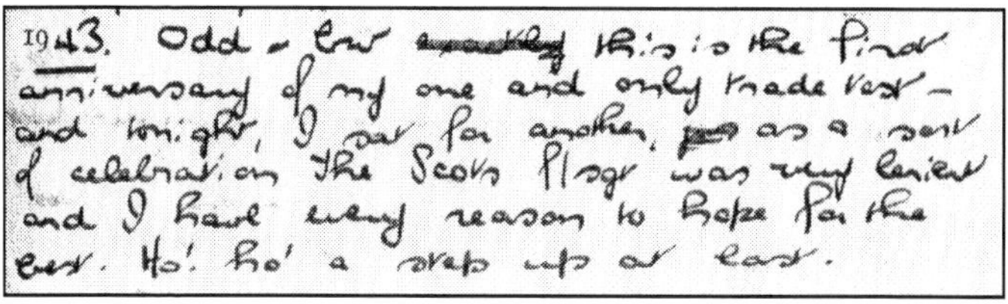
1943. Odd – but [illegible] this is the first
anniversary of my one and only trade test –
and tonight, I sat for another, [illegible] as a sort
of celebration The Scots F/Sgt was very lenient
and I have every reason to hope for the
best. Ho! Ho! a step up at last.

July 30th

Hostile aircraft overhead at the moment: Beethoven's First Pianoforte Concerto (being broadcast) gives me a sense of security and comfort that nothing but music could give. Somehow, it gives a feeling of permanence – of the eternity of things greater than man. I don't feel afraid.

1943			AUGUST			1943
M	T	W	T	F	S	S
..	..	..	..	..	..	1
2	3	4	5	6	7	8
9	10	11	12	13	14	15
16	17	18	19	20	21	22
23/30	24/31	25	26	27	28	29

August 2nd

At long last I am an LACW[1]. I didn't scrape through: did the job properly and got 91.5%.

August 4th

With several women and the Archduke to see a film. The A. returns to the bosom of his wife this weekend – thank Heavens.

August 5th

Michael is tired of battling and setbacks and desires only a life of peace and quietness, so – will I marry him? Wonder what gave him the absurd notion that I'd give him these things? His memory has failed him, it seems.

[1] LACW: Leading Aircraft's Woman

August 6th

Jerry writes and addresses me thus – "poor, withering WAAF." What ho! Attractive photo enclosed – complete with ears.

August 7th

With the lugubrious Doris to the Spa, where we met Frank and another cadet with whom we danced and laughed and drank coffee. I enjoyed it. Threw a tin of sugar at that man from Brazil this afternoon.

August 8th

Frank had an operation on his finger so sent a substitute to escort us to the concert. Horrified – and amused – to find myself falling very heavily for him. Fascinated by his perfect chin – and infuriated by his persistently contradicting everything I say. Meeting him on Thursday. His name is Jim Hewish.

August 9th

Mother is undergoing one of her periodic "I wish you'd get married" moods. Michael in hospital with burns and malaria. Have written a suitably sympathetic reply.

August 10th

To the "Drum" with Frank – who has adopted a most 'heavy Victorian father' attitude towards me. I can hardly wait for Thursday. Oh time! How it drags!

August 11th

Last date with the Archduke with whom I argued. He coldly informed me that he refuses to belief that I am a virgin: that it is impossible as only experience can be responsible for that certain look in my eye!

August 12th

Jim (the one for whom I've fallen so heavily) took me to the "Drum" and after a pint of weak beer, swept me out on the pretext of finding another pub. We sat in a field and kissed – I didn't expect it, but – I hoped it would happen.

August 13th

With Jim to a film. He and I are kindred souls – and I'd foolishly given up hope of meeting any here! Worships the sun and plans to travel. Feels that a little money is necessary but has no desire to work with one aim in view – to make money. Oh Jim! I can't help comparing you with Michael and loving you just a little.

August 14th

Jim and I were to see "Lilac Time" but he was confined to camp for some stupid thing. So I stayed in, looking around, washing things, and ironing a uniform that looked even more creased after all my efforts.

August 15th

Duty at the Abbey: Jim is on fire piquet[1] there.... All had a terrific tea – drinking session in the Abbey, and viewed the eclipse of the moon from Groupie's room. Ignored the moon as Jim was kissing me. Despite his previous accusation that I'd lost my chest, he now wants to kiss it.

August 16th

Heard from Donald Barrington several days ago. He's still not taking any part in this war. How can people adopt such isolationist attitudes? Tony Hinton with the R.A. in North Africa.

August 17th

Jim decided that we should go to a film. Collided with the Archduke and his wife: the A. looked very henpecked. Feel very frustrated: I was happily reconciled to the prospect of being made love to.

August 18th

Feel very depressed and irritated.

August 20th

To the Spa to get as stewed as possible. Chris Davies supplied whiskey which was promptly upset by another ASR type – very drunk. Chris sufficiently courageous to take me into a rhumba: also escorted me back to the Derwent. I like him.

---

[1] Fire piquet/picket – fire watch duty.

August 21st

Down to the harbour, where I was conducted over the Air Sea Rescue launch. Marvellous craft. Oh, what I'd give to go for a trip in her! Chris presented me with a packet of vile Brazilian cigarettes with a spot of good advice about not offering them to anyone I liked. Home by the afternoon train.

August 22nd

Lazy day with uncle Joe and the Pest on a fishing expedition. Total catch – four very small fish.

August 25th

Fishing – again: again, also, I didn't catch a thing – but neither did Leonard. Ha!

August 28th

With the Pest to a dance where one of his dainty cronies upset some hot coffee over me and I experienced the ecstasy of having me feet trodden on by a large sailor with flopping ears and a bald head.

August 29th

Spent the afternoon loafing on the quayside, rapidly acquiring the most decorative layer of coal-dust. Altho' the Pest insisted that my presence was essential he wouldn't allow me to do anything. I felt very smug when he caught a mere eel – total catch.

August 30th

With mother to Bournemouth to do the usual round - window-shopping, tea and a film - with just a little drink afterwards. Lengthy letter from Kay and a very charming photo of herself and a glamorous air-gunner who's done 400 hrs. op. flying.

August 31st

Usual mad rushing around and frantic race to the station. Train overflowing with children. Interesting to study them and decide how not to bring up my offspring. Spent an hour at the Abbey drinking tea.

1943			SEPTEMBER			1943
M	T	W	T	F	S	S
..	..	1	2	3	4	5
6	7	8	9	10	11	12
13	14	15	16	17	18	19
20	21	22	23	24	25	26
27	28	29	30	..	..	..

September 1st

And so to Worth. No sign of Jim as yet. I feel as though my happiness in the immediate future depends on him – and, him alone. The flapper, Eileen and I drank an enormous quantity of cider at the "Hole in the Wall". I felt temporarily uplifted.

September 2nd

Saw Jim from a distance. I took up my usual position at the window when his squad marched by. Was repaid by a very large grin.

September 3rd

Saw Jim at the "Thanksgiving" Church Parade. No sign of him at the NAAFI. Marched by at lunch-time and exchanged winks. To a film and a dance with Sheila this evening. Taken home by a cadet with slanting eyes. Didn't like him. Had to jump on his feet to make him release me.

September 4th

En route for the "Drum", met Jim who insisted upon our joining him and Basil. I was wildly happy at first but – awful anti-climax Jim made a bee-line for Sheila and I chased Derwent-wards, with Basil in hot pursuit. He consoled me but – I feel desperately miserable. How stupid – at 22! My faith in humanity has again been shattered.

September 5th

Awoke at dawn, feeling ghastly – can't decide which is worse – this ache for the Jim affair or the frightful taste in my mouth and – oh! my stomach. My sense of humour is asserting itself – and I can laugh – but how shakily!

September 6th

An amusing evening. Avenged myself by being extremely rude to Hewish (whom I'd invited to the WAAF party) and beetling off with Basil. Danced with numerous people but most of all with Basil, who is exceedingly dull. Such a shame – Hewish looked utterly miserable. Ha!

September 7th

Still desperately struggling against this ache for Hewish. Having some difficulty in maintaining a friendly attitude towards Sheila. Oh God! Help me to be civilised!

September 8th

I laugh more an' more. In retrospect, my emotional upset over the Hewish affair seems quite absurd. Italy has capitulated. I have an odd feeling that I'd like to go to church.

September 9th

Oh Heaven! How wizard. The Man from Brazil has asked me to celebrate. My patience and long-suffering worshipping from afar has been rewarded. It was a lovely evening – rum and whiskey and dancing at the Spa.

September 15th

WAAF Section, RAF Station Torquay: Parade commemorating the third anniversary of the Battle of Britain. (Dorothy marked with an inked 'x')

With Chris Davies dancing at the Spa. Oh Lor'! This man is fatal. I can find nothing to dislike, nothing to despise. His pleasant sense of humour – everything about him appeals. Good Lord deliver me from this tangle. I must not get involved. I must keep a clear head and not let my emotions and matrimonial instinct run amok.

September 18th

In civvies with Chris. To a concert given by a God-forsaken bunch of musicians who called themselves the National Symphony Orchestra. Escaped at the interval and didn't return. Got very merry on rum and returned to the Abbey at 20.30 hrs. Feeling very disturbed.

September 19th

Explored the Rock W but couldn't find my ear-ring. Met Frank who swept me into the Pavilion for coffee and a fatherly talk. Got cracking at midday, homeward bound.

September 26th

It's that man from Brazil again. As usual, we preserved the tradition of our drunken relationship by drinking rum at the Abbey. This man is fatal. The hitching round the world dream is fading more and more. My head must rule my heart. Damn Chris Davies!

September 29th

With Chris to the Spa where I changed into civvies. The foolish Chris muttering "Is there a preacher in the house?" Drank whiskey and gin with two Americans. The toast – "To Ohio and Illinois, Brazil and Dorset." Chris assures me that he has no intention of seducing me – but wants to marry me. Hell! I must remember – "Canada here we come". Damn Chris Davies!

1943			OCTOBER			1943
M	T	W	T	F	S	S
..	..	..	..	1	2	3
4	5	6	7	8	9	10
11	12	13	14	15	16	17
18	19	20	21	22	23	24
25	26	27	28	29	30	31

October 2nd

Chris and I drinking double rums and Pym's at the "Drum". Chris insisted on drinking to the future as he'd planned it. And I? – to the future that I'm fighting for – a losing battle, methinks. Damn Chris Davies!

MEMORANDA[1]

(Boyle), Penarth, Cardiff

KATHLEEN – Friendship began in June '40 when Kay & I were a coupla "rookies" beginning a new life – a wonderful life – at Andover, Hampshire. She is, I think the loveliest person I have ever met, and she seemed to be then, as she is still, a charming mixture of generosity, kindness, sympathy, gaiety and – tolerance. Our friendship has survived – through Andover, through Oxford, ever through months of separation. In January 1941, she left the WAAF and a few weeks later, was married to Billy Howe-Martin, Coastal Command pilot, whom she'd known for several years. South American Joe drove Hags Nos. 1 & 2 and myself to the wedding. In October of the same year, Billy was report as "missing over Norway". In November, Kathleen rejoined the WAAF – still hoping, still believing, still knowing that he was alive. K., is Hag No. 3 – a year older than I.

---

[1] Dorothy wrote a precis of important characters at the end of her diary and labelled them the "Memoranda".

JOAN (Ryalls) Prenton, Birkenhead

I met this old devil – now known as the Empress of the Hags" because of her great age (33 this year – whew!) – in the Andover days, too. For the first few weeks of our friendship, I had a sinister suspicion that she was very strait-laced and horribly prim and proper – and yet her eyes betrayed her. I guessed her past, even before she confessed – months and months later after innumerable beers in an Oxford pub. A few years ago she was engaged to a man, but she found his brother more exciting so she slept with him and married neither of them. She's a very calm sort of person and worries about nothing – thank God. In fact a woman after my own heart. Her brothers and sister are rather odd people too, especially Dick, who is a fighter pilot, and whom Joan describes as an "illegitimate father".

VIOLET (GOVER) Devon

Hag No. 2 has less personality than No.1 & 3, but without her, the foursome doesn't seem complete somehow. I met Violet at Andover, too. She is terribly vague and absent-minded and utterly delightful – specially in a "binge". The nearest V. ever got to being seduced was when a man once knocked on her bedroom-door!

(Dorothy – 1st Left)

(Dorothy – 1st Right)

(Dorothy – 1st Left)

War Time Photographs of Dorothy with WAAF Colleagues

Presumed to include the "Hags", but no formal and verifiable records can be found.

TONY (Hinton) London

This mad man of Magdalen is very long and has a beautiful chin. He's very clever, produces extreme plays which no-one understands and is reading history at Oxford, but his great ambition is to direct – or produce (forget which) films. He spends the vacs working in film studios in Town and is very kind to me when I meet him there. Inclined to be amorous, but he may grow out of it.

Anthony Hinton

Another of my dear mad men of Magdalen. Very amorous, painfully young and oddly attractive. Reading history but had a terrific ambitions to produce – or direct (I forget which) films. Worked in film studios during the long and frequent vacs. Met him once during a leave when he was at Ealing – cutting-room, I believe. Spent a weird evening drinking in shady little pubs and eating hamburgers. In Sept '42 I heard that the Army had nabbed him. Last seen the previous February. Just realised that this has all been written before. Ha!

MEMORANDA

EPILOGUE

The End of the Diary...

...though not the end of the story. Dorothy and Chris married on the 11th December 1943 in Poole, Dorset. Next follows some letters from Chris to Dorothy following their wedding:

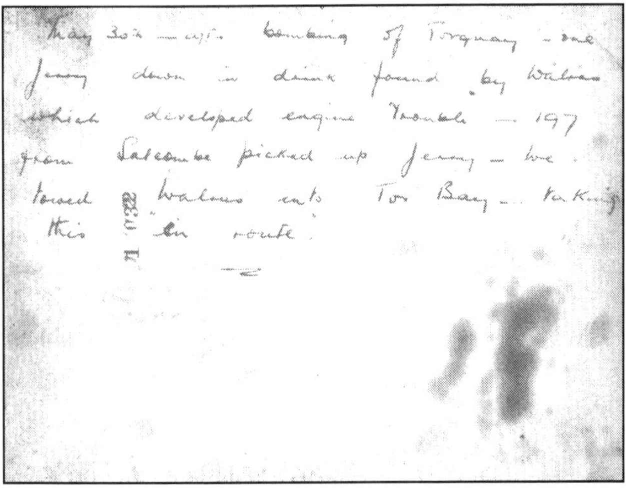

May 30th — after bombing of Torquay — one
Jerry down in drink found by Walrus
which developed engine trouble — 197
from Salcombe picked up Jerry — we
towed Walrus into Tor Bay — taking
this "en route"

A Message from Chris on the Back of a Photograph

Tuesday March 1944

Darling,

Another day's come and gone and another radio set working again. This makes four since I got back. Oh dear – the damned postman's being unkind – no letter from you yet. It makes me so peevish.

How are you darling? Recovered yet from the visit of that brute of a husband of yours? Take off that nose of yours darling and apply the catarrh clearing stuff won't you? I wish this ruddy business was all over and forgotten – a thing of the past – and that you and I were at last together forever. If only I could be patient – but it's no use- patience is a virtue I know I shall never again possess till the day of my final homecoming from this mob. Before I met you I always used to be glad to be back off leave. Not now, it's over a year since I knew any peace of mind or contentment at doing this job. Life's one long fret to be with you now, a fret that luckily has it's fairly regular spells of sublime contentment, wonderful you-filled seven day spells, spells whose only drawback, only snag, is that each succeeding one seems to widen the gap, & enhance the difference between life with you and life without you and makes me more miserable more dissatisfied with this makeshift war born empty existence than ever. Do I love you? Darling so very completely. Yes all of me, with absolutely no reservations and all, all of me is yours. I hope you feel as intensely about me as I do about you. I like to think you do.

It's not so cold now – very mild in fact. I think the bite has gone out of winter, though it may still have a nip or two in store when the March winds start blowing – if they are going to blow. It's still damp though.

I suppose Peggy will have gone back to Biggin Hill or Folkestone by the time you get this. I have been thinking about that estimate we made on how much it cost to keep the house running and think we ought to "up" our share to £2.0.0. at least. That is working on the assumption that it cost £5.0.0. a week to do the show & I personally think that Leonard should contribute 10/- towards it and have £1 a week to play around with. What does he do at the moment? Does he give all or nothing to his Mother? If nothing suggest this plan to him, (1) that he gives her

10/- a week, (2) that he starts a P/O. savings account and (3) puts in 5/- each week leaving him 15/- for himself. If he's willing tell him that I will start his saving account with £1 and give him in addition £2.10.0 to add to it every time I come on 7 days leave. All this providing that he stops pestering your Mother for money and in fact that he makes his 15/- a week do for what he needs. I think if he once sees a little bank account of his own, growing he'll start putting more than 5/- in weekly. I hope so. It might even make him look forward to my coming on leave.

This isn't philanthropy – just an experiment.

Goodnight now darling - I must write to Mother before I let it slide another day.

My life now is pretty colorless (Note American spelling).

Like me – it's you-less.

Yours Chris

X

700158 Cpl Davies

ASR/MCU
RAF
TORQUAY

Wed May 17th 1944

Darling,

It's your birthday – I hope it's been a happy day and that you've had a pleasant surprise or two. I remember as a child thinking that was what birthdays were for – pleasant surprises, and I still think that is their main function, and that the only reason why as we get older we enjoy them less is because we become harder to surprise each year. Or does that merely prove conclusively that I was a very spoilt child and had so much given to me that I eventually took everything for granted. I wouldn't be at all surprised but luckily fate stepped in when I left school and though I was still spoilt by parents, She, Fate, dealt me enough kicks in the pants to bring me back to a true appreciation of life and its pleasant surprises. And one way or another she continued to do that till last year when repenting she made you fall as I had done. And having learnt my lesson I knew that never again would I take king Fate for granted. This sounds incomplete. There should be a moral somewhere – but as it is I think that the embellishments it will do very nicely for the unknown quantity's first bedtime story "and the beautiful princess (that's you, Momma) and the prince of gnot-knees[1] (that's you poppa) were married and lived happily ever after." I'm afraid I shouldn't be any good at telling that one. I should be too tempted to tell how "on the way to be married, the prince and princess arm in arm, the brother of the princess, Leonardo, turned to the princess and said "Gee, Sis, you are a sucker." I shall never forget that and it still make me hoot with laughter every time I think of it.

I got your letter yesterday all 22 pages of, plus the supplement from South Africa and I loved it. It was a wonderful letter. I can suggest is that you send him a cable in return and

---

[1] Private joke, maybe?

sign it D.D. But I can't somehow see you doing this even if you know his address.

I haven't been to a film for nearly three weeks – they haven't appealed to me somehow but I should manage to get to see "The Girls he left Behind" which you recommended. It's showing here next week. "Bluebeards Eighth Wife" I saw a very long time ago and can only remember about it that Gary Cooper disliked intensely wearing either the top or bottom half of his pyjamas, I forget which.

Life seems to be rambling on pretty much the same as usual here though I think this disease, Secondfrontitis is beginning to get some of us down. We had our first (I think) case of a Cpl putting a bloke on a fizzer yesterday.

I'll write again tomorrow sweet these interruptions are too much.

I love you completely

Chris

Saturday August1944

Sweetest wife man ever had,

I got your lovely letter this evening, the one telling me of Wally's visit and about settling ITMA's bill (but you didn't tell me how much it was & I want to know), and all about Peggy & George. In similar circumstances my face would have been green.

Now about these Polyphoto enlargements I am going to be greedy of No. 4. I want one large one about the size of the one in what is now your bedroom – well it used to be there anyway. Of No. 42 I want just two postcard size & of 41 if it doesn't break the bank I want six postcard size or thereabouts. You made no mention of 22.

About Tony and Mary I don't think you need worry. He never had a chance to mean more than just a friend. I know that sounds very cold and matter of fact but you know what I mean – she won't have been so deeply hurt by it. She's had her share of that anyway when she lost her brother in Tunisia.

I was glad to hear Wally had called, and quite moved to think he'd saved £1 as a present for the twins. About the cigarettes I think it would be better if they were sent addressed to Wally, Ginger, Stan & Co in memory of happy hours at Torquay. I know they would all have loved to call if they'd been within calling distance which neither of the other two are.

The cheque for £10 from the R.A.F came as a big surprise to me. I didn't realize they paid prenatal allowance for each child – must have quads next time!!

Tonight I have been to see Olsen, Johnson in "Crazy House" another film I missed at Torquay. My only hope now is that they show "You were never lovelier" before I leave the island. Must find out if it's in their stock. They only have a certain number of films and from what I've heard these seem to go round & round in a vicious cycle.

Did you ever hear that old story of the Yank private walking in Hyde Park with a friend and saying:- "gee – look at dem boids". And his pal say "Those are birds" to which the Yank replied "Well, they choips like boids anyhow".

Darling it's coming up to midnight now so I'll close now and add tomorrow's effort later.

Goodnight sweet woman – I love you. X

Here it is Sunday. I cycled to Church this morning. The transport was u/s. it was a bit wet going through the mist and coming back against the wind was hard pushing but we made it and I was quite happy about it. It gave me some badly needed exercise. I was beginning to stagnate. I know just what you meant darling when you told Wally you'd left your Torquay brain behind. There was a time when I would mix it with the lads but long ago. Now I am just a passive and amused listener. I'll have to better myself.

I wonder do you remember Bill Towlson. I remember only one occasion when you met him & that was on one of our rare (?) visits to the Abbey Hotel. He was there with some of his crew. He was a Sgt then F/Sgt now. He's just moved in to our hut to fill the vacancy left by Stan's going. So that now we are four again.

Recently old Ivor Henry, the bloke the WAAF driver slung that crack at in Torquay, has been doing some pretty high powered boozing (he's like Dan & Tommy Plows, a returnee from a spell in Iceland) and the result has been several early morning scrambles to the lavatory just round the corner, waking us all up en route. So this afternoon, having warned Bill of this, we scrounged a bucket and stuck this on it:-

"Ivor dear, when this is near
Your nightly scufflings due to beer
We hope will cease
And give us peace".

Tommy Plows incidentally has already made a name for himself here. He is in a hut, one end of which is locked and one night he staggered in about 2 a.m. and went to bed waking up two hours later, with the same trouble he stumbled out of bed with a clatter and half awake started heading for the wrong end of the hut. People up that end immediately anticipating the worst sprang out of bed bringing torches into action to guide him out the other end. I think he just made it. But the lads are getting worried now. They don't feel it's safe to go to sleep when he's had a few.

Darling that's all for now - it's raining again - I wish I could be with you down there - I hope you're getting enough sleep.

I love you sweet Squiff

Goodnight

Yours Chris

Monday Oct 1944

Darling,

I didn't write yesterday – it occurred to me just after I'd posted my letter on Saturday that it wouldn't leave here till Monday morning, and that writing Sunday would mean two letters going by the same post so I foolishly allowed myself to be lured into a game of Housey-Housey in the N.A.A.F.I. which taught me just how foolish I was. An evening utterly wasted.

Tonight Stan leaves us and in about an hour I think I'll toddle down to this "spit and sawdust" boozer and have a drink to help him on his way.

Before joining this Housey gang in the N.A.A.F.I. last night I just caught the radio playing the loveliest version of "You'll be so nice" that I've heard yet Yes it was Dinah Shore and I just sat and listened letting the sentiment of it soak into me. Bad isn't it? But I did love hearing that song again. I always will.

You'll be paradise to come home to and love.

A lot of the quotations in this Sex book make sense. I like this one, it's from the chapter on "the valuation of sexual love."

"There is nothing real in the world but love. One grows tired of thinking, even of acting, one never grows tired of loving, nor of saying so. In the most tortures of affection I have never ceased to feel that the essential of happiness is that the heart should be worthily filled – even with pain, yes, even with pain, the bitterest pain."

Well we've agreed about that already when we hoped, not for a lifetime of everything we wanted but for a full life, a life of just the right mixture of sorrows to make the high spots really appreciated.

Another quotation, which sounds very like you a month after we were married. The effect of loving someone.

"One seems to oneself transfigured, stronger, richer, more complete, one is more complete. . ." I too felt it and still do.

Yes – it's funny reading this book and finding, in not quite the same words, the feelings we have expressed to one another, experienced and expressed by someone else.

The boat has just come in; I can hear its toot as it comes up the loch. I wonder will there be any mail on it for me?

Just remembered. If that parcel from Mother does arrive don't forget she's sent the dress lengths or something in it for you so open it and help yourself to chocolates too if it arrives.

You've said quite a few times recently how incredible it seems that the twins are ours, part of you and me. And yet you're with them all the time. I can hardly believe they exist, let alone that they're ours. Dear lovely lovable wife with twins,

Goodnight,

Keep fit and longing for our next meeting.

I do

Yours Chris x

Thursday (1945)

Squiff, my sweet,

Another letter from you, lovely you, today. The green paper was rather startling but darling there is absolutely nothing that could detract from the joy or minimize the kick I get out of your letters – sad state to be in. Yes – very sad. The longer we live this married life the more I realize that "it had to be you" and that no one else could ever possibly do.

This evening's come & my intention to spend it dashing around learning jigs & Highland flings and reels has been overruled by my natural laziness. I just can't be bothered. My mental slackness has spread to the physical side of me & now I'm in deadly (?) rut of not wanting to do anything but sit in the hut every evening writing letter and thinking of you.

I fixed up one of the units broken down P.S.I. wireless sets in the hut and now I can sit and listen to the A.E.F. programme or anything else that's on without going across to the mess. The height of laziness.

Washerwoman huh? Ok I had planned anyway to do my share of that when I get leave but I didn't realize your Mother or you were still being deprive of a lot of your sleep by the little blighters. I'll get leave now as soon as I can.

Proud poppa's feeding their offspring? I can just imagine the look of utter disgust on Ginny's face after half an hour of trying to get anything from my nipples.

I'm glad you liked the verse but it wasn't very bright and certainly not as bright as you made it out to be. There should be more coming if I could only de-stagnate this mental piece of mine.

Still heard nothing yet about the Harris Tweed. Any colour your Mother would prefer in case I get a choice? Better give me a long list just in case. The main sport here seems to be shooting rabbits. They go off at night to a place on the other side of the island 4 miles away armed with several guns and a long torch to shine on the rabbits. They brought back 16 (a poor bag!) the other evening.

Have you decided yet on which side to part Chris' hair left right or centre? What toothpaste is he using? And be careful what is said in front of them in case their first utterance is "bloody hell" instead of "Mummy" Ha!Ha! Pitfalls still to come. Bill wants to know if Chris knows the Morse code yet? I told him he belches in Morse and already knows how to send "Milko".

Well sweet you goodnight must dash off a letter to Mother now.

I want to hug you.

Chris xx

Friday

Just a note to let you know I'm back here O.K. (even though it is Friday 13th) and to say that it was a wizard crossing.

Hope to get your letters tomorrow morning.

I still hate you

Chris

Thursday 1945

Darling,

Money, birth certificates and envelopes and best of all a letter. Lovely girl – thank you: but you shouldn't have sent the extra pound or the envelopes. We have, (I thought I'd told you) a local G.P.O. and I can get everything in that line necessary.

And now cigarettes; please don't, for Pete's sake, send any. I get as much as I want in my quota from the N.A.A.F.I. without having to buy Capstans and I don't smoke Woodbines for economy sake any longer. I smoke them now because I prefer them. Yes it does sound strange – I'll admit that but it's true.

Thank you, sweet, for giving Ginny that middle name. I didn't like the thought of her blaming us in later years for any ragging, she might have had to go thru with initials of V.D. I like the name Ann too, but why choose it when you don't like it?

I shall send the birth certificates on to the Brazilian Consul and hope he will let us have all the documents he's got back together when my passport's straightened out.

Darling that's all I wanted to know – to hell with Havelock Ellis, and by so saying I suppose you know you've swollen my already inflated ego to bursting point. Yes sir I'm due for a fall.

I agree too that a discussion on Ten Sixty sex and all that between us would be rather comical. It's one of the many things we refuse to take seriously – and look what its landed you with.

Now – about this Harris Tweed, a further snag has developed in the form of an influx of Poles recently who have caused the price to jump. They seem to be as bad as the Yanks for this sort of thing. 'Tis rumoured they are even paying a shilling each for eggs. But apart from that – this Tweed business. You'll need at least 7 yards. But what I was thinking is this. Do you think there's any point in getting it when you'll probably never wear it after leaving England? I'll get some if I can but don't you agree it would be better to let your Mother have something made up from it, a coat or something? Finally don't send any money for it, in case I don't manage to get any. You won't get it till I come on leave anyway.

What you tell me about the Heavenly (?) twins is very unnerving. I think I'll have to take my leave up here, or wait till Christmas at any rate. Coward.

I had another letter from Ealing today offering sympathies for being so far away from Squiffy and the bairns. My uncle also had the ruddy sauce to say that he approves of Virginia but thinks Christopher should be Griffin Davies, feeling that he might find a double barrelled name useful in later life.

I think he was joking but it's too late now anyway. As if it matters whether he approves or not, though I think his suggestion for Chris Jnr good, but not for the same reason.

By the way I have just heard that there was a Scotch couple down at Cockington who were turning out Harris tweed double width but with coupons for 17/6 a yard & they tell me that ordinary machine loomed tweed on the mainland is 9/- a yard in any shop - but also with coupons. I shall proceed in search of it here in spite of all this and get some. They say the main snag (if you call it that) about our stuff is that it lasts forever and the costume is always years out of date before it shows any signs of wear.

Must go and do my last bit of washing before starting with Mrs Mckye,

Goodnight Darling,

Love you

Chris

Wednesday (16 months later) (April 1945)

My Squiff,

Yep - 16 months - and I'm still utterly and nattily crazy about you and missing you like hell and on top of all that, that 16 looks like being nearly 18 before I see you unless Father comes to the rescue.

I wonder how much longer I can go on putting up the pretence of being a perfectly rational sane, and safe being, under this system of only seeing you for four weeks in 52, one every thirteen. I thought I would become resigned to this way of existence as we move on but quite the opposite seems to be happening. I ????????? each separation less and less; miss you more and more each time I go away. I think if I have to spend another year like this I shall lose all that remains of my former good nature.

Today for the first time since I arrived back here I've had no letter, not that I expected one - the G.P.O. has very definite limitations. But I couldn't help hoping that one would come from you today, the 11th.

There's nothing to write about here. The girls in the Post office must have thought "swig-pigs" rather silly as they cackled like hens when I gave them the telegram.

The days are terribly....................................

Thursday, July 12th, 1945

Well, honey chile, here I am back in Glasgow again and the date is July 12, so I guess that means it's only four weeks ago today that I was here last on my way thru to the blasted isles.

I left Inverness at 11 am this morning and arrived here about an hour and a half ago – just after 5 pm, in one of the heaviest showers of rain I can remember.

Finished "Strange Fruit" last night, the blurred vision passed off very quickly. A combination of poor printing and my habit of skipping bits here and there meant a lot of re-reading for me. The way it's written you can't skip at all without becoming confused and losing the thread of the story. I think almost every character suddenly switches back into odd bits of the past. In one or two places where bad printing has left no gap where there should have been a gap I've put in a series of inked dots. I'll send it on to you when I get back to Loch B.

Thought of you a lot in the train today – you of the lovely legs, the colour of your eyes. I feel such a terrific surge of emotion whenever I think of you – a sort of welling up inside of me of something I can't describe – and it makes me so damn impatient and irritable. Darling I do love you so very much. I wish the Air Force would stop footling around and would do something about getting redundant trades released. But of course that wouldn't help me. I would have to be a w/om.

Four weeks since and I can't at present see me coming on leave till Sept 15th at the earliest – maybe later. That's at least another 9 weeks yet. Gosh, I feel furious about it.

Darling, on your recommendation I think I will now dash out and see "Something of the Boys."

Goodnight darling
And Ginny
And Chris Jr
Yours (very Snr)
Chris

Thursday (1946)
Darling,

Here it is dance night again and I've just finished ironing (?) what I washed yesterday. Just as well I did wash them too for irony of ironies today we, up here in Britain's heaviest rainfall area, are without water. The pipeline burst last night & for the time being all washing of any kind is forbidden till the damage is repaired. I just managed to get my evening shave in before the restriction came into force and brought a bucketful of water to the hut anticipating it.

Alfie Leigh's letter is still down at the section – I really must remember it tomorrow.

By the way please don't bother to send up my shoes. If I still feel like learning these Highland dances in a few weeks time (and it will have to get a lot colder before I do) I'll bring them back off leave.

Harris Tweed. I was shown 4 samples today and choose one for your Mother but I think it will make a better coat than costume; and it will be for this that I shall wire you for money tomorrow. I think it should make a nice present for her.

I had a letter from Aunt Lottie this morning which came with a muffler she had knitted for me. She passed her 93rd birthday in September still calls herself "an old partridge" and repeats the gem about her little dog and the parrot. I definitely must take you up to see her before we go out to Brazil.

I am writing tonight to Mrs Howard at Blackpool asking her if she would send my trunk on to Poole addressed to 175. It should arrive just about the same time as I do, if I know anything about it, and I can deal with it and tip out all the superfluous junk.

Well, how are you, sweet? Still coping? Still bearing up under the strain of all the spare time you don't get now? I'm full of beans again now – cold sore completely disappeared & my only worry is that I still haven't got used to writing letters with people nattering round me. After the peace and quiet of my little old room at the top of Beacon House this place often seems like a madhouse; so that when, as yesterday & the day before, all four of us are in the hut all evening its more than I can do to write even my ordinary letter. So I look forward now to seeing the two drinking types wend their way barwards after dinner at night. It means that – I'd better start again. It means I can concentrate on and really imagine myself to be with you and telling you these things instead of writing them. And writing while a natter is going on seems like two conversations crossing at a table.

Well darling tonight I'm with you and I don't have to try and shout down someone else's chatter. Darling I love you.

Mother' s letter readdressed from Torquay & a parcel containing the Portuguese Grammar & one of these Teach Yourself Portuguese things as I shall have plenty to do if all I do is to concentrate on these. Roll on the long winter evenings. I shall be writing you in Portuguese soon.

Well, Stan is with us no more – they tell me he had so many beers last night he was in two minds as to whether he'd go or not (he's very stubborn after he's had a few) but they finally managed to get him aboard.

I joined them down at the Lochboisdale Hotel for a drink and then came on up to have a bath and bed. Well – good luck to him. He said he'd look the twins up whenever he's in Poole but somehow I shall be surprised if you write to say he's paid you a visit.

By the way thank you very much for the telegram. I wonder what the hell, if anything, will follow it. I'll bet Mother has packed up another parcel already. She says in her letter today that she'd got your letter thanking her for the nappies & etceteras and only wishes she could have sent more.

I do hope the war ends & we can go home soon. I do want to see all the old places & faces, and to see you surrounded by them (places – not faces) and happy there.

Meanwhile goodnight sweet Squiff

God bless Mummy, Daddy, Chris & Ginny

I love you, squaw

Your little old Big chief

Chris

On July 3rd 1946, Chris and Dorothy, Chris Jr and Ginny sailed from Liverpool to Buenos Aires, Argentina. They stayed in a hotel there and a few days later flew to Rio de Janeiro, Brazil, staying at the Copacabana Palace Hotel. The young family were met by his parents, Chris's sister and friends. Yes, the future looked rosy and promising.

A third baby had been made in England, and would be born in Matozinhos, Minas Gerais.

More to follow in Volume II...

ACKNOWLEDGEMENTS

Photo Credits:

All photographs reproduced here were taken personally by Dorothy, Chris and their friends and are from Virginia's family personal collection. Used with their permission.

~*~

Cover photograph of Dorothy – Retouched and colourised by user "Caz" of Rootschat.com; used with her permission.

~*~

September 4th 1942, RAF Form 252: Presumed to be Crown Copyright – date of original unknown.

~*~

November 9th 1942, RAF Form 1250: Presumed to be Crown Copyright – date of original unknown.

~*~

September 15th 1943, Parade photograph: sharpened and contrast enhanced by the members of Rootschat.com and used with the Board's permission.

Design & Typesetting

David & Karen Slee for ARC Publishing. Fonts under license. Original artwork by David Slee.

ABOUT THE AUTHORS

Dorothy Griffin (Diary Author)

Dorothy was born in 1921 in Poole, Dorset, the eldest of three children. She was beautiful, impulsive, courageous and amusing. Her accent was not a "Darzet" (Dorset) one, but that of a well-spoken English person. This she acquired at the age of 11, when a new girl arrived at her school, so she copied the accent.

Dorothy "Squiffy" Griffin joined the war effort in the WAAF and her no-holds-barred diaries of her experiences during WWII demonstrate that in more modern times she would be described as a hell-raising socialite. Dorothy married and left for Brazil with a young and growing family.

Dorothy returned to England at intervals from 1951 to 1977. Her husband Chris passed away in 1985 in Niteroi, Brazil. There followed a long gap of 17 years, when in 1994 she returned with Chris Junior for the celebration of her first-born twins' joint 50th birthday.

During a period of 35 years Dorothy corresponded regularly telling stories about the family, her employers, the political setup, the corruption, the Jogo do Bicho and the Esportiva (Football pools).

Dorothy's war-time diaries and letters came to light in 2001 in Niteroi, Brazil, following her death in England. Members of the family gathered at her home in Niteroi to pay their respects. Chris Junior became custodian of the diaries and letters together with photographs and other documents. Her daughter Virginia Dickinson was privileged to see these in 2004 during a visit and in 2009 Virginia's twin brother allowed her to borrow the diary and letters and Virginia hastily transcribed their contents to ensure their preservation.

Virginia Dickinson (Editor)

Virginia was born in Poole, Dorset in 1944 to Chris & Dorothy Davies (née Griffin). The family moved to Brazil in 1946, where they lived on a cattle and plantation farm in the state of Minas Gerais. In 1960 the family moved to Niteroi, the city over the bay from Rio de Janeiro. In 1966 Virginia travelled on the R.M.S, "Arlanza" to England planning to stay with her maternal grandmother for a year. Cupid had other plans as she married and had a daughter.

Over the past fifty years Virginia has collated the family photos, documents and the stories therein and plans to publish the collection as a sequence of events – a social history. This will enable future generations to view their heritage through Virginia's window to the past and will be especially relevant to those residing in Brazil and interested in their English surname.

Armed with her mother's war time diary, father's letters, and other family correspondence, Virginia felt the need for further research to find the family connection and draw to Brazil and this has taken Virginia and her partner Raymond Slee to Austin, Texas, to The Lincoln Archives, The British National Archives, down a redundant (disused) gold mine in Minas Gerais, and The Anglo Ashanti Museum in Nova Lima, to name just a few locations exotic, and less so. The research so far has uncovered enough material for at least four books. And so, Virginia decided to start with Mother's Diary and Father's letters from WWII forming this Volume I: "The Man from Brazil".

INDEX

A

B

C

D

E

G

65151275R00098

Made in the USA
Charleston, SC
16 December 2016